Praise for *Strange Frequencies*

"With all human culture arguably evolved from Paleolithic shamanism, Bebergal engagingly explores the uncanny overlap between an ancient landscape of occult ideas and today's techno-saturated environment, from Victorian table-tilting to the digitally remastered voices of the dead; from confidence tricksters, through the desperate or delusional, to the artists and visionaries currently exploring this marvelous, ectoplasm-damp material. An absorbing, comprehensive guide to the high-definition séance parlor of the modern world, and a timely reminder that, in contemporary civilization, we are never more than a couple of centuries away from an alchemist."

—Alan Moore

"Even the most well-read esoteric scholar will find some new and fascinating bit of lore in Bebergal's book. . . . an engrossing read . . . And as far as tour guides to the occult underworld go, you couldn't ask for a better Virgil than Bebergal: his prose is warm, clever and erudite without being alienating. Read it with as open a mind as he wrote it and you'll be bound to pick up a few interesting frequencies on your wavelength."

—*Fortean Times*

"Bebergal dives into the relationship between technical and occult imagination and comes up with something profound about the human experience. By turns funny, spooky, thought-provoking, and moving, *Strange Frequencies* is brilliant work."

—Daniel Abraham, *New York Times* bestselling coauthor of the Expanse series

"This enchanting, insightful book equates the effects of diverse phenomena from Elizabethan stagecraft, cybernetics, and handmade automata and the Brazen Head to astral travel and ectoplasmic

T0005934

manifestations—and examines them all in light of the human hunger for a magic that may be far closer to us than we know."
—MARIA BUSTILLOS

"Bebergal deftly explores how we subliminally or overtly use science and technology to rediscover the evolutionary metaphysical heart of what it means to be human, and our desire to speak with voices no longer bound to the Earthly plane."
—J. H. WILLIAMS III, *THE SANDMAN: OVERTURE, PROMETHEA, ECHOLANDS, BATWOMAN*

"In these technology-haunted times, we are sorely in need of a guide for the perplexed limning the connections between our eternally seeking souls and our gadget-addled minds. Peter Bebergal is the ideal companion on this quest, finding ghosts hidden in the machines all around us. *Strange Frequencies* is a delightful and engaging examination of the human desire to forge new keys to unlock the mysteries of life."
—PETER MANSEAU, AUTHOR OF *THE APPARITIONISTS*

"Ever dream of building a monster in your basement? Photographing ghosts? Entering drug-free states of euphoria? You're not alone. In this brilliant, knowing, and thrill-a-page historical and literary exploration, Peter Bebergal explores the human endeavor to use technology to probe hidden and forbidden zones. *Strange Frequencies* expands how we understand technology and takes us into shadowy realms where science and strangeness intermingle."
—MITCH HOROWITZ, PEN AWARD–WINNING AUTHOR OF *OCCULT AMERICA* AND *ONE SIMPLE IDEA*

STRANGE FREQUENCIES

THE EXTRAORDINARY STORY
OF THE TECHNOLOGICAL QUEST
FOR THE SUPERNATURAL

PETER BEBERGAL

A TarcherPerigee Book

tarcherperigee

An imprint of Penguin Random House LLC
penguinrandomhouse.com

First trade paperback edition 2022
Copyright © 2018 by Peter Bebergal

Illustration on page xiv courtesy of Steve Banes; illustration on page xxxiv © Mark Podwal, in the collection of Jewish Museum in Berlin; photograph on page 14 © Nico Cox; illustration on page 36 originally appeared in Theodor Eckardt, Die Physik in Bildern Eßlingen, 1881; photograph on page 72 © Shannon Taggart; photograph on page 104 © Unknown press photographer. Collection Friedrich Jürgenson Foundation, courtesy of Carl Michael von Hausswolff; photograph on page 136 © Ronni Thomas; photograph on page 168 © Joshua Madara; photograph on page 196 © Peter Bebergal

"The Golem of Boston" originally appeared in a slightly different form in *Berserker* #1, Breakdown Press, 2017

Most TarcherPerigee books are available at special quantity discounts for bulk purchase for sales promotions, premiums, fund-raising, and educational needs. Special books or book excerpts also can be created to fit specific needs. For details, write: SpecialMarkets@penguinrandomhouse.com.

THE LIBRARY OF CONGRESS HAS CATALOGED THE HARDCOVER EDITION OF THIS BOOK AS FOLLOWS:
Names: Bebergal, Peter, author.
Title: Strange frequencies : the extraordinary story of the technological quest for the supernatural /
  Peter Bebergal.
Description: New York : TarcherPerigee, 2018. | "A TarcherPerigee book." | Includes bibliographical
  references and index. |
Identifiers: LCCN 2018018498 (print) | LCCN 2018028356 (ebook) | ISBN 9781101993071 |
  ISBN 9780143111825 (alk. paper)
Subjects: LCSH: Parapsychology—Research. | Spiritualism. | Supernatural. | Occultism. |
  Technology—Religious aspects. | Religion and science.
Classification: LCC BF1040 (ebook) | LCC BF1040 .B37 2018 (print) | DDC 130—dc23
LC record available at https://lccn.loc.gov/2018018498
p. cm.

ISBN (paperback) 9780143111832

Printed in the United States of America
1st Printing

Book design by Daniel Lagin

For Amy and Sam, the electrical current that powers my heart

Contents

Symbol / Circuit / Sigil

I n the June 1956 issue of *Astounding Science Fiction*, the same magazine that introduced L. Ron Hubbard's *Dianetics* to the world, editor John W. Campbell described the Type One Psionics Machine, also known as the Hieronymous Machine. Patented by Thomas Galen Hieronymous in 1949, the device is a tool for focussing one's psychic abilities—a bridge between magic and technology of the sort that Peter Bebergal eloquently describes in this book.

The Hieronymous Machine seems designed, above all else, to confound our expectations and preconceptions about not just technology, but reality itself. Even its inventor had to admit in his patent that while "the apparatus functions . . . the principal upon which it is based is not fully known." Campbell had initially set out to ridicule the device, but was shocked to discover that it worked—something he ascribed to human "psionic," or psychic, abilities, rather than to the technology itself. To demonstrate this, he built a streamlined, "symbolic" version, just a circuit inked onto paper, like a magical seal, and found that it worked just as well as the electronic model. "The machine works beautifully," he wrote to Hieronymous, "the consistency of performance is excellent . . . we're working with magic."

Some years later, rocket engineer Harry Stine discovered Campbell's symbolic Psionics Machine and, determined to show that Campbell had been hoaxing his readers, built one for himself. At first, to his relief, it didn't work, but he then noticed that Campbell's printed circuit had omitted a key filament connecting the vacuum tube to the rest of the device. Stine drew in the missing filament; and suddenly the machine worked. In his 1985 book *On the Frontiers of Science: Strange Machines You Can Build*—a firm favorite of William S. Burroughs, who championed his friend Brion Gysin's Dreamachine, described within these pages—Stine credits the Hieronymous Machine with curing a debilitating outbreak of warts that his daughter was suffering from.

And suddenly we are outside of time. . . . Wart charming was, and still is, one of the traditional services offered by the cunning, or wise, women and men found, since the dawn of human culture, in communities the world over. It works, and always has done, provided that both parties have somewhere within them the capacity to believe. For Stine and his daughter, his drawing of the Hieronymous Machine was the tool that completed the human circuit and allowed magic to flow between them.

Just what that magic might be is one of the mysteries explored within these pages. You will have heard Arthur C. Clarke's aphorism that any sufficiently advanced technology is equivalent to magic for those who don't understand it; equally important however, is the awareness that any sufficiently advanced magic is, in itself, a technology, one that, fuelled by the caster, converts magical potential into magical force that can affect the world around us.

As "technomancer" Joshua Madara explains in this book, a good magician works with the scepticism of their audience, using this, rather than stage dazzle, to confound and surprise them. This state of tension—questions rotating, at the speed of thought, around a core of uncertainty—dramatically amplifies the potency of this-might-be-magic, creating an engine of enchantment akin to the Alternating Current motors developed by Nikola Tesla, the patron saint of technomancy.

If we consider magic to be the ability to inhabit, manipulate, and eventually exteriorize one's imagination, then Tesla's ability to visualise, in three dimensions, the workings of his inventions—as would-be Golem-builders are instructed to by the *Sefer Yetzirah*—is the perfect illustration of what Peter is exploring here: using magic to develop technologies to make magic with. The symbolic circuit is now fully inked.

No book of magic would be complete without a warning to the curious. In James Blish's 1968 novel, *Black Easter*, a nihilistic arms dealer employs a cynical warlock to unleash the forces of Hell on Earth. The arms dealer does it to make money; the magician just wants to see what might happen. As I write, an uncannily similar situation is playing itself out in our newsfeeds: curious data-sorcerers, employed by mercenary dealers in weaponized information, have been using social media, our technological collective unconscious, to hack and manipulate the political opinions of millions of people in order to shape global events. This is black magic in its purest form, and its consequences could well prove catastrophic.

We must re-learn to defend ourselves against these psychic attacks and, where possible, to fight back. You will find timeless strategies for doing so within this book, in the desire and generosity of its author, and its intriguing cast of characters, to share both their magic and their insights into the contemporary imagination, and the yawning unknowns at its core.

There is no time to waste—that process starts *now*. So disconnect your computer; charge your soldering iron; chalk out your circuit board; build your Dreamachine—and let the dance of light consume you. It is time for the conjuration to begin.

Mark Pilkington,
Wiltshire, England,
Spring 2018

Panel from "D-E-V-I-L on Your Dial," from *Adventures into the Unknown* #42, April 1953 (American Comics Group), pencils by Dick Beck and inks by George Klein

INTRODUCTION

"It's a Transmitter! A Radio for Speaking to God!"

I am a TV baby. One of my earliest memories is watching the moon landing with my mother on the television set in my parents' bedroom. The next day, Monday, July 21, 1969, the *New York Times* headline read "Men Walk on Moon" and the accompanying article called it an "Ancient Dream Fulfilled." The day before, then President Nixon spoke to Buzz Aldrin and Neil Armstrong in their command module and congratulated them, saying, "Because of what you have done the heavens have become a part of man's world." The image of men on the moon beamed across space and onto that little black-and-white screen was a miracle almost as grand as the "ancient dream" of touching the divine. Technology made both miracles possible.

There was also a color TV in the den, and I can still recall the strains of the closing song from *The Lawrence Welk Show* as my parents carted me off to bed. From *The Brady Bunch* to *Love Boat* to *Happy Days*, Saturday morning cartoons to *H.R. Pufnstuf* to reruns of *Batman* and *Star Trek*, late-night monster movies and *Saturday Night Live*, the television saw me through childhood into adolescence. It was the hearth of the house for myself and many others in the 1970s and early 1980s. It made sense, then, that in the 1982 film *Poltergeist* directed by Tobe Hooper, the angry, confused ghosts would find their way into the Freeling family home through the television set. With the famous gleeful announcement by the late Heather O'Rourke: "They're here," the most ubiquitous piece of technology in American homes became the gateway for the spirit world into the suburbs of America. Technology was not only the medium for the message, it was the medium for the spirits themselves.

It wasn't at all surprising.

From modern-day tools used to contact the dead to humanity's age-old use of machines and incredible devices to probe the unknown, technology has been used for centuries to bridge the gap between the material and the mystical, revealing that the workshop and the séance parlor have more in common than we might think. Despite the seemingly secular power that technology provides, at every step along the way we trafficked in our spiritual concerns and our religious needs. It was not enough to be able to send a telegraph over the ocean or almost two centuries later to have a video chat on our smartphones. The former would become a metaphor for Spiritualist mediums who believed they listened for spirits that might be lurking along those very frequencies, and with the latter we devised ways to hunt for poltergeists with a ninety-nine-cent smartphone app. Blending our technological ingenuity with a belief that our spiritual destiny need not struggle against scientific innovation is a unique expression of our humanity.

It was my television-watching generation that would embrace and become enthralled with the merging of technology and the great mysteries, an advance into the future for us in both mind and spirit. It was through the television that I first understood that for all their expression of our rational scientific progress, our technologies are forever imbued with a sense of the otherworldly. But ours was not the first generation to link them. The 1933 Plew Television Ltd. advertisement introduced their TV sets by announcing: "IT IS HERE," a remarkable transmission from the past heard in the Hooper film. The ad goes on to describe its Model No. 1: "The magic eye . . . the enchanted mirror . . . The fantastic dream of ancient witches who were burnt for their dreaming." As early television technology developed, even its faults were characterized with the lexicon of the supernatural, as in the case of the "double-images" that the media scholar Jeffrey Sconce explains were called "ghosts . . . wispy doubles of the 'real' figures on the screen." So, when the ghostly skeletal hand emerges out of the screen in the Freeling parents' bedroom in *Poltergeist*, Hooper was simply making literal the metaphors we had become accustomed to. Moreover, it might be that some part of us never fully trusted the strange technology of the television to begin with, our ancient superstitious brains convinced there was something supernatural in its very working. Hooper's film was also making these fears manifest.

Our visions, our inventions, and our terrors are not always easily separated. This was particularly palpable during the 1970s of my TV-radiated childhood. The youth culture came kicking and screaming out of the 1960s, looking behind them as their dream of an Aquarian Age utopia was reduced to LSD casualties and drug addiction, a war that no amount of protesting seemed to be making any impact on, and gurus seemingly all becoming murderous cult leaders, their followers mere sycophants rather than enlightened avatars. There were pockets of hope, and some were simply disappointed the psychedelic eschaton had not been fulfilled. There was a danger the future was presented as spiritually bereft, but a window had been opened that looked toward the east for enlightenment and wisdom. The culturally alternative practices of hippies and rock stars soon became mainstream. In the mid-1970s, meditation, yoga, and words like "karma" and "dharma" were part of the vast spectrum of everyday spiritual activities.

It was during the 1970s that the popular culture consciousness began to incorporate terms like "occult," "supernatural," and "paranormal" into its lexicon, which captured a kind of spiritual meaning, and yet remained incredibly fluid. The "occult," for example, took on the quality of something slightly sinister, the dark workings of a black magician or a Satanist. Most forms of religious or spiritual beliefs that existed outside mainstream Judeo-Christian norms became subsumed under the terms "occult," such as magic, tarot cards, astrology, witchcraft, and even Ouija boards. At the occult's heels is the "supernatural," a word that typically included ghosts, poltergeists, haunted houses, life after death, and demonic possession. The paranormal, while often inclusive of supernatural themes, tended toward human potential, for example, telepathy, telekinesis, and other psychic phenomena (and in the 1970s might even have included strange goings-on such as sightings of Bigfoot and the Loch Ness Monster).

The darker trends of magic and mysticism also resonated for the younger generation coming of age in the 1970s. Satan seemed to love making his mark on youth, inhabiting poor Linda Blair as Regan in *The Exorcist* and ensuring his reign reborn as the shifty-eyed Damien in the *Omen* films. Classic monster movies were dug up from their graves and became part of the regular TV diet for many kids on local channels, myself included, while we flipped through the pages of comics like *House of Mystery*, *Chillers*, and *Monster on the Prowl*. Heavy metal bands were finding a shout to the devil had teenagers swooning, parents worrying, and albums selling.

The television set now became a crystal ball to divine the way to our spiritual anxieties. An earlier generation had watched *The Twilight Zone*, a show that illuminated and dissected their own fears of communism, alien invasions, nuclear war, and conformity, but 1970s popular entertainment seemed much more concerned with the state of our souls. In the made-for-TV movie *Devil Dog: Hound from Hell*, Satan finds a way to seduce the perfect (TV-watching) nuclear family by way of their loyal German shepherd. Paranormal powers and cryptozoology were investigated on *In Search Of*, narrated by the calming voice of Leonard Nimoy, a jolting dichotomy of the irrational presented by the figurehead of logic and reason. What made *In Search Of* unique was that it gave the appearance of rigor, of a cogent investigation of the weird. The subjects—Atlantis, ESP, UFOs, the Loch Ness Monster (my personal favorite)—were subjected to a certain level of scrutiny. These glimpses into ancient and cosmic mysteries through the lens of science offered a guilt-free way to enjoy the weird and paranormal, along with a nudge toward the suspicion that there was something true about these claims. *In Search Of* often presented the stories as if the public was only now becoming privy to truths long known and accounted for. Indeed, some of us were hopeful that our generation would usher them in, shine the light on the secret history of the world. Nevertheless, to avoid suggesting that aliens are actually among us or that plants have feelings, the show opened with a voice-over disclaimer: "This series presents information based in part on theory and conjecture. The producer's purpose is to suggest some possible explanations—but not necessarily the only ones—to the mysteries we will examine."

INTRODUCTION

While the dark side of the occult and paranormal painted popular spiritual interests in lurid colors, something was stirring in our collective dream for better things to come. In 1975, it was certainly marvelous that you could play Pong on your television and then in a few short years play a host of video games on the Atari 2600. But it was just as wonderful that you could build a computer from a kit. In the 1970s, ham radio usage was starting its decline, but the home-inventor slack was being picked up by a renewed interest in hobby electronics, partly made possible by the abundance, and affordability, of integrated circuits. It was the spirit of invention and innovation coupled with the mystery of what was possible that had me poring over Heathkit catalogs and electronic hobby magazines, and taking apart—and not always successfully putting back together—every electrical gadget in the house. The same year the Apple II computer was introduced to the home market, Heathkit was offering a computer in kit form. The division between consumer and builder had not yet been severed and indeed it was out of that generation of electronic hobbyists that the next wave of computer technology would arise.

Like the language used to imagine the men on the moon, and the arrival of the consumer television set, this tinkerer sensibility is linked intimately to the religious impulse, as well as to our supernatural imagination, which extends away from convention and hierarchy toward risk and individuality, which might also make it a very Western capitalist cultural movement. Technological innovation only strengthened the sense that we were in charge of our own destiny, be it physical or spiritual. Even a subset of the hippies understood this, despite their communal foundations. Not only were the 1960s alternative religious phenomena an attempt to wrestle God away from the mainstream religion and dogma, it was also a call for direct and immediate spiritual experience, mediated independently, be it through LSD, meditation, or magic.

In 1968, the *Whole Earth Catalog* birthed the do-it-yourself (DIY) culture—the very things that would inspire Steve Jobs and Bill Gates—that was the first real holistic attempt to merge what might at first seem like two opposing forces: an organic spiritual vision dedicated to the natural world and a global electronic future that propels the human being toward technological transcendence. The *Whole Earth Catalog* was a phone book–sized tome, a curated directory to herald in a techno-utopia: books on geodesic domes, computer building, dolphin intelligence, and mushroom hunting shared pages with recommendations for calculators, self-hypnosis techniques, science fiction novels, and meditation cushions. In the first edition published in 1968, editor Stewart Brand writes, "We are as gods, and might as well get used to it." In an interview with the *New Yorker* in 2014, Brand describes the difference between those who used LSD to change their spiritual consciousness, and those who used it to change their technological consciousness. Brand saw the *Whole Earth Catalog* as the manual for the latter, a counterculture that would change the spiritual condition of the world with computers and new sources of energy. His vision would plant the seeds for cyberculture and the hacker movement later, both attempts to seize whatever measure of control they could from those in power. This movement would also presage an idea that technology could aid in our spiritual growth.

I was too young to have gleaned any inspiration from the *Whole Earth Catalog*, and instead it was a much smaller cultural artifact—a simple line of dialogue from a Steven Spielberg film—that would insert itself like an earworm into my unconscious. In the 1981 film *Raiders of the Lost Ark*, Indiana Jones's archrival René Belloq pleads with Jones to try and understand his obsession with the lost Ark of the Covenant. For Belloq, the desire to claim the vessel that contained the Ten Commandments was more than a mere archaeological wonder. Belloq seethes, "It's a transmitter! A radio for speaking to God!" Here indeed was a deep and unyielding truth: as we entered a truly technological age, we would be impelled to look back at ancient forms of magic and occult practice and imbue them with this same kind of technological purpose. Spielberg was plugging into a current that had been running through film and other media for decades. And like many others, I couldn't let go of the idea that the world of magic and spirits would somehow tag along with us. I couldn't let go of the irrational even as the rational was building a new world before my young teenage eyes. I was watching the future arrive more quickly than I had imagined possible.

We've never been able to let go. This impulse to use technology—if only metaphorically—to engage with the spirit world is deeply rooted. As we'll see, this desire manifested in the legend of the golem, in the hidden workings of automatons, in the quest to photograph spirits, and even in the earliest ideas of Spiritualism that sought to unify belief in spirit communication with the explosion of scientific knowledge and technological inventiveness. We tend to view this as an intersection of mutually conflicting forces, one rooted in the rational, the other rooted in the irrational and superstition.

The persistent idea that science and religion are opposed is a fairly recent phenomenon. While certain ideas were suspect during the Middle Ages, it really wasn't until Charles Darwin and Sigmund Freud reversed long-held assumptions about human beings' place in the cosmos that the tension boiled over. Darwin taught that we are not separate (souls) from the animal kingdom but in fact part of a lengthy process inside nature's crucible. Freud cast away any demons or original sins that made us behave in terrible ways, instead showing, that like Darwin did with our species, our psyches are also products of evolution, but only as old as the moment we were born. This attack on human beings' primacy, and our divine origins and futures, created a rupture in the natural sciences.

Many early alchemists, naturalists, and scientists saw their task as the work to uncover the secrets of the divine will using a rational and exact examination of nature and natural phenomenon. Species of animals and plants, fossils and shells, could be classified showing an ordered relationship between them. This relationship was understood to be a manifestation of God's mind. The nineteenth-century scientist Louis Agassiz, who founded Harvard's Museum of Comparative Zoology in 1859 (it officially opened in 1860), the most important research museum of its time, was a deeply religious man who fervently believed that nature was evidence of a divine creator. He once wrote: "The combination in time and space of all these thoughtful conceptions exhibits not only thought, it shows also premeditation, power, wisdom, greatness, prescience, omniscience, providence . . . and Natural History must in good time become the analysis of the thoughts of the Creator of the Universe."

As the rift between faith and science became more and more divisive—particularly after Charles Darwin's publications on evolutionary theory and Sigmund Freud's psychoanalytic revolution—religion began to steel itself to protect some of its fundamental ideas that were under attack from all angles. Religious thought, particularly in the Protestant sects, started to use the language of science and scientific methods to *prove* religious ideas. On the other side, the scientific community became more and more uncomfortable by the religious sentiment in its own history, blaming the new literalism of religion as distorting scientific language. For example, the early writings of naturalist John James Audubon are filled with what one might call religious or spiritual feelings, but contemporary bird guides are dull and static by comparison, as if any sense of awe or wonder has been stripped clean, like the feathers from a bird. But the spiritual impulse remains.

A person turning on a light switch to illuminate their home does not need to understand the theory of electricity to make use of the technology that exploits it. For the nineteenth-century Spiritualists, for example, technology that used electricity, such as the telegraph, was believed to have corresponding devices in the spirit world. In this way, technology could be applied to any spiritual question because the underlying scientific theory could be dismissed. More important, technology can be thought of as a mediator, in the religious sense of the word, an Earth-made vessel through which human beings can relate to the uncanny, supernatural, or divine. As scientific knowledge advanced, certain religious communities sought to be more rational in their claims of how the environment and its inhabitants reflected religious dogma.

Radio communication, first realized with the telegraph, ignited the imagination, in this case as a potent metaphor. Cromwell Fleetwood Varley—a nineteenth-century engineer and one of the principal technicians involved in laying the transatlantic telegraph cables—was a foremost mesmerist and Spiritualist who believed that his work with telegraph systems and electricity offered methods to understand how the spirit world interacts with the physical. His work would presage an entire Spiritualist and occult culture that sought interactions with supernatural entities and magical forces via radio, devices known as spirit trumpets, and even the idea of a mechanical ear that could listen in to the conversations between angels.

Our technological ascendancy, however, does not always come about as grace. Many believed that divine power was something that must be wrested from heaven as when, in 1840, the Unitarian minister John Murray Spear believed he was visited by a group of spirts, among them Benjamin Franklin, who provided instructions on building a machine that could harness divine energy and power every other machine in the world. In this case, technology provides a dual function: it is technical knowledge that the spirit world communicates, and it is God's method of acting directly on humanity. No mere miracle, Spear's machine had its basis in real-world engineering and science. The proof of supernatural forces and the existence of spirits lay in its very construction. Spear's machine provides a useful metaphor for human beings' confidence in technology. But the general public was even more amazed at Nikola Tesla and Thomas Edison, two men who showed that technology, unlike the laws of nature, can bend to the human will. Technology gives a sense of control, a means by which human beings, through their own resourcefulness, could exert influence over the mundane—and the ineffable.

Early-twentieth-century creationists tried to show how the Grand Canyon was evidence of a great flood, and later proponents of intelligent design claimed that the human eye was a perfect machine that could only have been crafted by a divine hand. But creationism was the outlier. For most, science was ascendant, and while religious institutions maintained a vital role in people's lives, technological progress was of a different domain. People were content with the separation. Sometimes, though, those pesky spiritual metaphors intruded. A decade or so after World War II ended with the annihilation of Hiroshima and Nagasaki, Harry Truman said that he had no regrets about making the decision to use the atomic bomb: "The atom bomb was no 'great decision.' It was simply another powerful weapon in the arsenal of righteousness." This was merely an amplification of what he had told the American people in his 1945 address immediately after the bombs fell: "We may be grateful to Providence that the Germans got the V-1's and V-2's late and in limited quantities and even more grateful that they did not get the atomic bomb at all."

With every successive technological advancement, we imagined still greater progress, but we clung to a set of questions—of hopes—that I don't imagine we will ever abandon: Does God exist? Are we more than physical beings? Is there a spirit or soul that persists after we die? Is there anything beyond the phenomenal world? Even when we pragmatically turn away from these questions, they continue as ideas to explore in art, literature, and film. They endure because in these questions we find a way to enchant our lives. Technology does not, and should not, necessitate that we abandon this quest. Instead, our technological innovations are potent metaphors keeping these spiritual explorations alive. But they also become literal tools through which to experiment the boundaries of the physical world and our own psyches. These fantastic accounts of spirits and aliens riding into our lives via electric currents were not so strange to the people who were experimenting with technology in the hopes of talking to spirits, transcending the limitations of their physical bodies, and using technology to imagine and demonstrate the creation of life.

Science is built on testable theories that require certain controls, and continually points to a stable physical world whose laws are consistent, measurable, and often predictable. Quantum mechanics has posed an entirely new set of questions, and at the quantum level, particles behave in ways that don't always square with physical reality. Even so, quantum effects are not replicable in the macroscopic world. Technology—a direct product of scientific principles—can be made to produce effects that contradict those very principles, such as taking photographs of spirits or communicating with the dead over radios. On one hand, ghosts, aliens, and occult powers of the human psyche— ideas outside of the realm of science—are given a rational underpinning when viewed in the context of technology. This is good news for the charlatan who will use technology to "prove" that they can hear messages from the astral plane, as their marks will believe that an iPhone application can pick up messages from the dead because it was programmed using those methods of science. On the other hand, we have not yet solved the problem of consciousness, which allows for wild speculations that cross the wires of religion, science, the supernatural, and technology.

The riddle of consciousness—how it arises, whether it is merely a complex chemical reaction in the brain or if it exists via some other mechanism, does it remain after death—is a principal mystery dogging many who have exploited technology to unravel, often using devices in ways far outside their intended purpose. These methods include radios tuned to unused frequencies in an attempt to speak to the dead, cameras that take photographs of spirits, machines thought to be imbued with souls, and gadgets intended to harness divine power, to become as gods ourselves. In other words, with technology we have unendingly struggled to define the limits of consciousness, and our mortality.

At the time of this writing there is life on Mars. It's in the form of two robotic rovers—Spirit and Opportunity—but their synthetic lives contain what is most vital about humanity. Within these two-thousand-pound technological marvels is a dream that humanity has been having about itself for centuries. It is the dream of extending ourselves out into the universe, to behold our origins, and to sow the seeds of our immortality. Back on Earth, we still are having the same dream, but here we are sending ourselves through the digital ether, augmenting our bodies with smart watches, virtual reality glasses, and synthetic limbs that can respond to brain activity, and developing artificial intelligence in the hopes that some part of us might live forever. In the light of all this astonishing technology, it would at first appear that the need for spiritual meaning has been dissolved. Built on the clean slate of science, technological innovation has exposed the irrelevancy of myth and religion, and, by extension, of God. Nevertheless, it is this spiritual yearning that has not only made these advances possible, but has oriented them toward a particular aim: our immortal soul's communion with the divine. More important, the very desire to master our environment, to feel some modicum of control in a sometimes-chaotic universe, and to expand our mortal condition derive from our fundamental belief in a spiritual destiny. It is not merely about living forever. The desire for immortality is an existential spiritual condition. It is about perfectibility, a divine inheritance. Whether trying to divine our futures, communicating with spirits of the dead, or becoming gods ourselves, the quest has always been the same. It was once called magic, the seed of all religious practice. Now we use technology toward the same ultimate goal. Even as humanity created technological wonders, our desire to connect to a divine principle was not eradicated. Instead, technology reshaped and re-enchanted our connection to our divine inheritance.

So, for me, it seemed that going native was the best, and riskiest, means of exploring these extraordinary technological wonders. In writing this book, I sought out, engaged, and worked with individuals who currently are attempting to use technology for spiritual ends. Through the resurgent DIY culture known as the maker movement, I also found myself witnessing how technology could offer a new set of tools for breaking open the spiritual and occult imagination, as well as that deeply human drive—to commune with the divine in an effort to search for our own immortality. This also means having to engage with notions and beliefs that are so often associated with the irrational, the unscientific, or the just plain foolish. But the metaphysics or ultimate truth of these ideas is not so relevant as how they have, for centuries, prompted human beings to excite their imaginations, to glean meaning from the antipodes of thought. To this end, it means using those pesky mercurial terms like "occult" and "supernatural." For the most part, I will use the colloquial meanings of these terms and will adhere to their (wildly) shifting definitions. What is normally called "paranormal," however, will not make much of an appearance here, as I am mostly concerned with those ideas and beliefs that have some spiritual or religious dimension built into their DNA. For this reason, mediums who claim to speak to spirits will feature prominently, but a psychic who believes they can see into the future with their mind alone will not. And while I am going to be investigating things that closely bump up against scientific principles, I am purposefully avoiding those areas that have been the subject of methodological research, like ESP and near-death experiences.

My path ahead is one that offers no answers to the great spiritual questions, but it does illuminate how technology—rather than make these questions no longer relevant—underscores how deeply they inhabit our imaginations. It begins in the realm of artificial life and ideas of the soul with an attempt to build a golem and other artificial constructs. The road winds deeper into the dense forest of magic and Spiritualism, where stage magicians and mediums plied their trades using many of the same techniques. I follow the Spiritualists in their attempt to capture the soul of the dead in a photograph as well as learn from a contemporary photographer a surprising truth about this desire. Later, the spirits of the dead will continue to call to me from inside radios and other devices meant to listen in to their secret conversations in the ether. Eventually, I will meet tinkerers and inventors who are trying to supercharge their own spiritual destiny with strange machines. Finally, I'll get my hands dirty (and solder burned) as I attempt to make my own occult and supernatural technologies, following the guidance of hackers old and new.

My investigations and engagements with the practitioners I meet allow me to explore the psychological and personally spiritual dimensions that technology offers. I wanted to answer these questions: How can magic function as a metaphor for craft and handiwork? What will happen if I do indeed encounter what seems to be a voice from beyond? And if I don't, will it increase my skepticism or simply provide a different set of tools for asking those questions—inquiries that may never truly be answered? I soon discovered the essential historical moments and characters that have prefigured their modern equivalents. They begin in ancient Greece, with stories of mechanical constructs built by the gods and the medieval golem, extend to the development of automaton (and subsequent questions regarding the soul), and find their hallmarks during the invention of the telegraph, the camera, and other moving picture techniques. Along this continuum, what became most apparent to me is that nontraditional modes of religious practice often ask the questions that the mainstream communities cannot. Technology is simply another underpinning of the vibrant intersection between our spiritual concerns and the culture at large.

I also found a need to reinvest our cultural language about technology with spiritual metaphors in order to find a meaningful and authentic way to create a bridge that connects our material with our spiritual concerns. An absence of any true spiritual language to engage with technology is detrimental to a mindful and imaginative future. What propels scientific inquiry if not the imagination? And yet imaginations are often haunted by loss. Ghosts, and where to find them whether they are real or not, are still symbols of our deepest need to connect our world, with one that extends beyond us, toward an immortal soul. And our world is undoubtedly a technological world, growing more complex with each generation. But I needed to start somewhere, and like many travelers before me I thought it best to consult an oracle.

Computers and the Internet have made a kind of magic that works with a simple mouse click. Literally, hundreds of websites, programs, and smartphone applications function as digital divination devices. The I Ching—the ancient Chinese oracular system made up of sixty-four hexagrams, stacks of six lines either broken or unbroken—is now available in digital form. The traditional method of casting a hexagram usually employs throwing three coins or sorting a bundle of yarrow stalks, techniques that randomize each of the six lines of a hexagram. While writing this book, I visited the website Eclectic Energies, which offers a hexagram generator by "throwing" virtual coins. Before I clicked on the "throw" button, I meditated for a moment on the writing of this book. The resulting hexagram was "Sun/Penetrating Wind," which reads: "Persistence brings good fortune. / Aversion goes away," for which the authors of the site offer the following interpretation: "Carrying an action through to deal with a difficult situation. This is no problem, one just has to make a start, and keep in mind that this is taking some time." Any writer during a project would happily receive this augury. The times in my life I have physically rolled the coins and looked up the resulting hexagram in a text, such as the beautiful 1950 I Ching translation by Richard Wilhelm (with a foreword by Carl Jung), I entered the frame of mind that requires us to be receptive to the oracle. Using the website, however, that ambiance was missing for me, but it didn't prevent me from accepting the message and meaning of the hexagram. Of course, behind this serendipitous moment was a bit of computer code, a programmed randomizer. Is this kind of virtual sortilege different in any way from doing it manually? What makes a computer program "occult" is its ability to plug into the elements of our consciousness that recognize the intent and output as preternatural. These are old archival tapes that we continue to store, not in the cloud or an air-conditioned warehouse dug into the foot of a mountain range, but archetypes and mythologies that stimulate our spiritual and occult imagination.

The supernatural and occult imagination becomes the locus where the tension between the material world and the world of the spirit is realized and is then dissolved. Pop culture is only one arena that empowers every desire and every anxiety regarding a supernatural reality. Even as music, film, novels, and comics are the perfect vehicles to practice spiritual rebellion and engage with that part of the human experience that desires a direct encounter with the divine, the occult imagination is also the location where superstition, conspiracy theories, and fear of the demonic manifest. The occult imagination is vast. It not only includes our desire for divine knowledge, but encompasses the fear of that knowledge. To commit heresy necessitates a universe that can be profaned. Then there are the more cynical uses of the occult imagination involving those who have duped others into believing in supernatural forces. But the occult imagination is also one that sees these beliefs and practices as folly, either dangerous, duplicitous, or self-deluding. Nevertheless, it is not necessary to believe in life after death or divination or any kind of miracle to engage with the supernatural. Even when we turn our attention to these ideas in order to debunk them, we are still participants. We give them life by asking the questions.

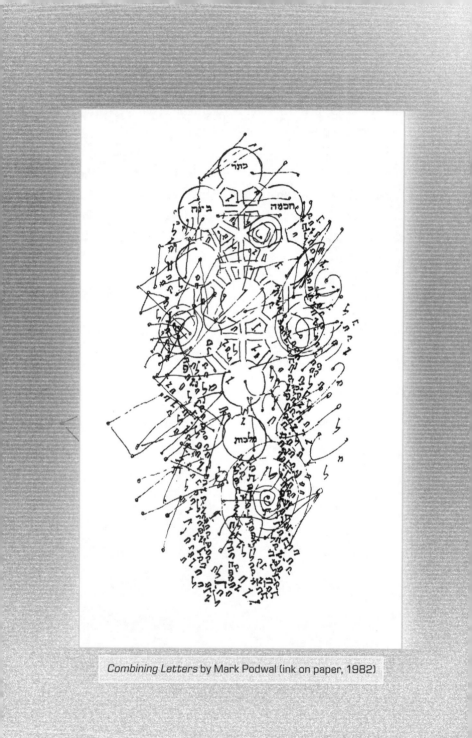

Combining Letters by Mark Podwal (ink on paper, 1982)

CHAPTER 1

The Golem of Boston

I knew that attempting to create a golem was going to be difficult. To build a golem—a clay figure brought to life by divine magic—first requires a mastery of ancient and medieval Hebrew. I can recite the Aleph-Beit, I can recognize the letters in a prayer book, and even sound them out slowly during a Yom Kippur service, but unfortunately, I never learned any more than what was required for my bar mitzvah, almost four decades ago. And even if I get up to speed on the rudiments of the language, there is a still greater obstacle: reciting the 97,240 permutations of the combinations of the Hebrew letters (yod-he-vov-he) known as the tetragrammaton, the name of God believed to have been given to Moses on Mount Sinai. This magical formula—found in the ancient Jewish text the *Sefer Yetzirah*—is the source code, the divine programming language that not only powers a golem, but was believed by Jewish mystics to be the script that runs the universe. My proficiency in Jewish mysticism is akin to knowing three commands of BASIC ("INPUT," "GOTO," "PRINT"). The attempt, nevertheless, illuminated how and why the golem has become the most compelling metaphor for acts of magical and technological handiwork that is also a microcosm of the divine creation.

My very first encounter with the golem legend came long before this recent investigation in a Yiddish tale "The Golem" by I. L. Peretz, translated by Irving Howe, in the collection *A Treasury of Yiddish Stories*, which sat on the bookshelf in the den of my childhood house. This version of the famous legend tells of the pogroms in the Prague ghetto getting worse and worse until one day the people urge Rabbi Judah Loew (usually rendered in Howe's translation as "Loeb"), the great scholar and mystic, to help them. In an almost matter-of-fact tone, Peretz describes the rabbi going out into the town, gathering up some mud, and forming it into the likeness of a man, and then he "blew into the nose of the golem—and it began to stir; then he whispered the Name into its ear," and the golem went out of the ghetto and began slaughtering the gentiles. Eventually, the Jews of the ghetto thought this was taking things too far and begged the rabbi to stop the golem. Loeb recited a prayer, "whispered into its ear," and the golem became a lifeless hunk of clay. There are several variations, most notably those where the golem is not destroyed but rather made inert, its body hidden in the attic of Loeb's synagogue.

At the time, this story was as close to anything I had heard of in myth or legend that resembled my singular childhood obsession: the Frankenstein monster. Saturday morning Creature Features had introduced me to James Whale's original 1931 version and all the Universal film sequels (*Bride of Frankenstein, Son of Frankenstein*, and yes, *Abbott and Costello Meet Frankenstein*), as well as the later and more lurid Hammer studio remakes, such as *Curse of Frankenstein* with Peter Cushing and Christopher Lee. That the monster was oddly innocent always troubled me. His creation was an abomination, a body without a soul inhabiting its frame. Further, it was not the power of God that ignited the monster's spark of life. Weird science coupled with Dr. Victor Frankenstein's mad ego turned man into a corrupted deity. Victor, played by Colin Clive in the 1931 film, calls out, in the moment he sees his creature move its hand for the first time, "Oh, in the name of God! Now I know what it feels like to be God!"

Loew's golem in the Peretz tale, as well as other versions, didn't have the same grotesque origins as Frankenstein's monster, which seemed to me at the time simply a contraption, a kind of bulky machine or weapon whose specific purpose was to protect the Jewish people from those that would seek to destroy them. Frankenstein of the movie created his monster not as a tool or even as a helpmate, but out of wild hubris, his face mad with power as he notes the monster's hand twitch and cries out, "It's alive, it's alive, it's alive!" What I noticed even then, however, is that the monster made of dead body parts and Loeb's heap of clay brought to life do share one thing: the zeal residing within each of their creators—the desire to create, to turn lifelessness into life itself.

The next golem in my life was found in the 1978 edition of the *Advanced Dungeons & Dragons Monster Manual*, a catalog of creatures great, small, and terrible, to be used by a dungeon master to populate their caves, crypts, tombs, and forests in a fantasy role-playing campaign. Nestled between the entries for "Goblin" and "Gorgon" is "Golem," described as "magically created monsters . . . The creation of a golem involves ultra-powerful spells and elemental forces." The *Dungeon Masters Guide* of the same game offers the "Manual of Golems," an artifact a player desiring to make a golem would have to acquire. It is said the character must "not be interrupted" when studying the manual, and there is a chance the golem will "fall to pieces" immediately after being constructed, echoing the original Jewish legend. But what is most remarkable about the game's instruction on the golem is that only a character known as a magic-user should attempt to use the book. A cleric—a class with a religious proclivity and whose power arrives from a deity—will suffer tragic consequences attempting to make a golem. The subtext here, reflecting 1978 American cultural fears about overplaying our technological hand, is that the construction of a golem is an irreligious act, one that requires the use of arcane and infernal *magic*, as opposed to *divine* power.

It seems remarkable that 1970s role-playing underscores an essential element that is not found in the tale I had first read about the golem of Prague. There, Rabbi Loew performs an act that is not described as magic, and does not involve any ritual more complicated than simply writing a word on the forehead of his lifeless lump of clay. In fact, as the Jewish scholar Moshe Idel notes in his seminal 1990 work *Golem*, Rabbi Loew's students and followers never referred to the golem in their own writings about their teacher. Loew was not a magician, and likely did not believe that magic was an appropriate subject of study. While Rabbi Loew is the single most famous maker of a golem, any occult aura was redacted from the well-known legend.

Certainly, Dungeons & Dragons wouldn't be my starting point for attempting to build a golem, but neither was the story of Rabbi Loew. This version of the Yiddish tale did lead me to others that offered more instruction, or at least a method that has likely changed in the telling over time. One detail is consistent, however. The golem is imbued with life by inscribing the Hebrew word *emeth* (truth) on its forehead (or sometimes placing a scroll on which *emeth* is written into the golem's mouth), and is turned back to a heap of clay by reducing the word to *meth* (death) or by invoking the name of God. The magic is intrinsic in the words, not in any special activity of the rabbi. In the legend, when the word or name is removed, the lifeless clay tumbles to the ground, crushing the rabbi to death.

Tales of the golem tend toward two themes. The first is that the name of God has been forgotten, symbolized by the inert mass of clay hidden in the attic of a synagogue. When we were closer to God, we knew his name and were privy to the secrets that bring about mystical understanding, which in turn can be used in service of *tikkun olam*, the reparation of this broken world. The second is that in trying to create life, the rabbi has exceeded his bounds of creative gifts and the result is his being crushed by his own creation. The golem becomes an image of dangerous pride. A similar lesson is taught in one of the only (and earliest) references to the golem in a Jewish canonical text, a curious tale found in a section of the Talmud known as the Sanhedrin, discussing various forms of magical practice. The text says: "Rabbah created a man, and sent him to R. Zera. R. Zera spoke to him, but received no answer. Thereupon he said unto him: 'Thou art a creature of the magicians. Return to thy dust.'" That speech is a vital aspect of life and is a nimble way to distinguish between the creation of Adam by God and the creation of a golem. Adam is not a golem, even though they are made from the same elemental material. Further, Adam can speak. The golem in the Talmud is mute, a magical con mimicking life but not equal in any sense to a human being created by God.

Subtle magical elements can be found in any number of golem stories. In an early version of the legend described by Jakob Grimm from 1808, the golem is found in the city of Chelm, where it is not a rabbi or mystic, but simply the "Polish Jews," who are privy to the divine secret of God's name, which they use to animate their golem. Grimm also inserts the notion that building a golem can be dangerous. Here, the golem grows larger every day, until it becomes an uncontrollable walking heap. When the secret word is erased by one of the residents of Chelm, "the whole load of clay fell on the Jew and crushed him." In writer and illustrator Mark Podwal's lovely children's book retelling the Prague story, *Golem: A Giant Made of Mud*, the narrator admits that "How [the rabbi] brought the figure to life remains a mystery," but that either a "piece of parchment bearing God's name" was placed in the golem's mouth, or it was "Hebrew letters he inscribed on the golem's brow that gave it life."

It took a non-Jewish telling of the tale to add up all the pieces of the legend's magical motifs and create what would become the default and most popular idea of the golem. The less Jewish the source, it seems, the more magical the tale becomes. In the hugely influential silent 1920 film *Der Golem*, or *The Golem: How He Came into the World*, the German director Paul Wegener introduces us to Rabbi Loew of Prague, who is told that a decree has been signed banishing the Jews from the city for their blasphemous religious practices. Loew struggles with how to respond, but soon decides that he has power to save the Jews. In one of the most detailed magical rituals portrayed on film, Loew calls upon the demon Astaroth, who appears as a monstrous ghostly face. Loew beseeches the demon, who reveals a secret word in smoky letters—"aemhet" (a rendering of the Hebrew *emeth*), which Loew writes down on a small scroll and inserts into a clay seal in the shape of the Star of David. Here, the rabbi is certainly more magician than *tzaddik* (holy one). Loew proceeds down to a secret lair, a necessary accessory for any wizard or sorcerer, where we see charts and diagrams with measurements and other magical formulas. He unveils a huge clay statue and affixes the seal to its chest. At large in the city of Prague, the living golem saves the royal family from a collapsing ceiling, and as thanks, the Jews are reinstated as citizens. But all is not well. The demon comes for his payment for the secret word and possesses the golem, causing it to wreak havoc through the streets. The golem is eventually put to rest by a golden-haired girl who removes the seal from the creature's chest. It's not entirely clear what the moral of this version is exactly. We are meant to feel sympathy for the Jews, but it's obvious that Loew's decision to use magic is dangerous folly. That the innocence of the perfectly white Christian child saves the day invokes some of the root notions of anti-Semitism. Naturally, this tale of the golem becomes the popularized telling, and even makes an appearance on *The Simpsons* anthology episode "Treehouse of Horror XVII" in the story "You Gotta Know When to Golem."

From all these tales and imaginings, I learned the most important thing: a magic word or a holy name was what I needed to make a golem.

The *Sefer Yetzirah*, thought by some scholars to be as old as the second century, is one of the most inscrutable texts in the history of mysticism. It describes in deeply symbolic language how God went about creating the world, operating a long series of thirty-two paths or processes that include, along with the twenty-two letters of the Hebrew alphabet, what are called the ten *sefirot* representing the unownable and ineffable of God's attributes that interact with creation. The *Sefer Yetzirah* is both a map and a blueprint for creation. Often rendered as a diagrammatic tree, the *sefirot* are connected to one another via the twenty-two letters. This is the scaffolding of all creation.

According to the *Sefer Yetzirah*, God "engraved," "carved," "permuted," and "weighed" the letters and created "all that was formed, and all that would be formed." Medieval kabbalists such as Rabbi Eleazar

Rokeach (often referred to as Eleazer of Worms) developed formulas for how the various letters should be combined to mimic God's creation of human beings, albeit in a much lesser form. His and other techniques typically involve taking "virgin" or untilled soil, mixing it with water, and forming it into a figure of a person. Specifications are not provided. But as we saw, golems have been known to be very, very large. To create one, you must first build the creature in your mind, limb by limb, head to toe, holding the mental image while reciting the appropriate sequence of letters that correspond to each part of the body as laid out by the *Sefer Yetzirah*. "Assuming that one can pronounce four syllables a second," Aryeh Kaplan writes in his translation and commentary, "it would take approximately seven hours to complete this entire process," with another formula taking possibly up to thirty-five.

There is debate regarding whether the creation of a golem was a magical activity intended to create a literal artificial being, or a mystical procedure to bring about an ecstatic state—less about the external object as an extension of divine power and more about an inner transformation. The thirteenth-century mystic Abraham Abulafia's method, for example, incorporated intense breathing exercises and physical movement toward the purpose of inducing an altered state of consciousness. Gershom Scholem, the preeminent scholar of kabbalah, also writes that the golem served to prove the magical acumen of the creator, a kind of initiatory ritual that, once complete, would allow them access to even greater divine secrets.

The seeming impossibility of making an external or internal golem given the almost superhuman formulations required for either left me to wonder if, outside of the legends and the complex kabbalistic commentaries, anyone has attempted to make a golem. Hoping to find at least one contemporary example, I reached out to various scholars and other experts, but no one knew of any nonlegendary accounts of someone who even claimed to have done so. Nonetheless, I was certain there would be one living kabbalist who had at least heard a rumor or other anecdote of even an effort to create an animate embodiment of the divine creative spirit, even if only in the form of an ecstatic thought form.

There are modern occult practitioners engaged in the creation of "magical servitors," what a commenter on an online occult forum defines as a "symbolic representation of a simple command." This can often be an aspect of one's own psyche being given autonomy, often with a start and end time, to help manifest a desire. Fred Jennings, part of the Brooklyn, New York–based occult book shop Catland, described them to me as autonomous sigils, self-creating symbols of intentions. To create a servitor, as we saw with the golem, the magician will inscribe an image or form in their mind and imbue it with instructions, but there is no real material component such as a clay figurine. The writer and magician Phil Hine gives the example of a commonly used servitor called "ICANDOO" (to wit, "I can do") as a thought form "to assist those who used it for overcoming any obstacles that crossed them." Jennings explained how it is helpful to think of a servitor as a piece of computer script, written by the programmer to initiate a certain task without having to be manually run. But a servitor can also be projected onto a totem of some kind, like a statue or other figurine, and in a way creates a physical object that "holds" the entity and provides a more concrete focus for the practitioner. These were not the golems I was looking for.

After months of searching for someone who would be willing to talk to me about golems, I was able to connect with Rabbi Eyal Riess, director of the International Center for Tzfat Kabbalah in Safed, Israel.

Speaking by phone, I could tell immediately he was less interested in the golem itself than he was in what the legend teaches about the divine, in particular how the Hebrew letters are the schematic for creation. Starting with Abraham, he told me, some people knew the secrets of the letters and the powers inherent in them, which, as kabbalists believe and the *Sefer Yetzirah* describes, is what God used to create the world. "And so, wise men of different generations knew how to use these godly powers of creation in the letters to . . ." The rabbi paused and then continued, ". . . to sort of create." And creation, he said, is "bringing something into existence out of absolute nothingness." God, he told me, used the Hebrew letters to not only create but to imbue plants and animals, "every entity," he emphasized, with the spirit of life. And certain people who knew the secrets of the letters could follow the formula to create a golem.

Rabbi Riess was insistent that the golem is not an ecstatic magical practice, but the intentional religious act to create an actual living being that would, if necessary, protect the Jewish people from danger. I was startled that the only Jewish kabbalist I could find who was willing to speak with me about the golem insisted that the golem of Prague was real and not an "ecstatic performance or experience." For hundreds of years, he said, a select few could perform such a miracle, but this was because there was a special need: Jews were being persecuted and killed in pogroms. The belief that the golem was a magical procedure intended to produce a mystical experience was anathema to Rabbi Riess. "The golem wasn't created for fun or for practicing something," he told me. "It was not someone saying, 'Let's see if we can do such a thing.'"

He was not unsympathetic. Instead of attempting to create an entity outside of myself or within my own psyche, the rabbi offered this exercise: "Look at your own body and feel like a golem yourself." The purpose of the *Sefer Yetzirah*, he believes, is not to learn how to develop the creative power of God, but to meditate on the "the godliness in day-to-day life." When you look at your own hand, he explained, you should be amazed at the complexity of it. "How does the spirit of life that I have inside of me," he urged me to ask, "enable me to move my fingers, my arm—to feel the skin, this blood, this warmth, this mechanism?" The creation of a golem is the recognition that the human being *is* the "magical anthropoid" created by the divine. "Right now, right this second, God is providing life to me." Indeed, humans' historical quests to re-create life without sexual union, ignoring the body, is a tradition for another scholarship.

Passover would be starting in a few days, and so Rabbi Riess, in perfect Jewish teacher form, used the example of the matzah to explain further. "This little cracker, a bit of dehydrated wheat, is able to connect my soul to my body." The Hebrew word for wheat, *chita*, he told me, has a numerical value of twenty-two, the number of letters in the Hebrew alphabet, which, as we now know, is the stuff the world is made of. "The matzah represents the power of life connecting body and soul through the letters. This is how to meditate on the golem."

The golem, it seems, is not merely a magical man conjured by a wizardly rabbi, a crafted wonder, but a gross representation of the human being as God's own handiwork, as well as an act meant to distill God's own creative power where he "formed a man from the dust of the ground and breathed into his nostrils the breath of life, and the man became a living being." The novelist Michael Chabon, writing for the *Washington Post*, offers that "Much of the enduring power of the golem story stems from its ready, if romantic, analogy to the artist's relation to his or her work." Even more germane is that the golem had once been a means for achieving ecstatic devotion to God, and today the golem is a metaphor for what the scholar Kevin LaGrandeur calls "the power of special knowledge." The golem lives as a metaphor for technology, particularly artificial intelligence, not only as a direct comparison regarding the creation of artificial life, but the danger that can come if we lose control of that creation. The heavy clay may come tumbling down on our heads. The image of the golem has extended into our own understanding of our creative capacity. But like the golem, even the smartest computers are limited in that they can only perform the function they are programmed to do, no matter how adept they might be. A chess-playing computer is very good at playing chess, but it can't decide not to. Similarly, a golem can be understood as "a big moving automaton," despite how anthropomorphic it might appear. It is mute, incapable of independent thought, and in the story of the golem of Prague, deadly to the enemies of its creator. In 2015, the physicist Stephen Hawking made the dire prophecy that artificial intelligence will usher in the end of humanity. In an article for the *Forward*, Benjamin Blech connects Hawking's warning to the golem: "The story of the golem of Prague is a paradigm for the hazard of permitting what we create to go far beyond our intent."

There may never have been an actual golem, nor even an attempt made to fashion one. Nevertheless, it was an idea that grabbed hold and continued to make its way through history. The golem is about ourselves, our spiritual and technological capacity, but it is also about our limitations. The golem is also an essential piece of magic technology, something that we enchant as a means of revealing the secret nature about the divine. Of these golems, I found—hidden in abandoned synagogues, teased out of the pages of impenetrable texts, monsters crushing their enemies, or a spiritual metaphor for my own mortal machine—none explained how the story of the golem had reached across centuries to remain the persistent image of the human being's desire to create artificial life. I would have to locate another instruction manual for building a golem, but instead of clay and holy letters, I would use gears and magic words.

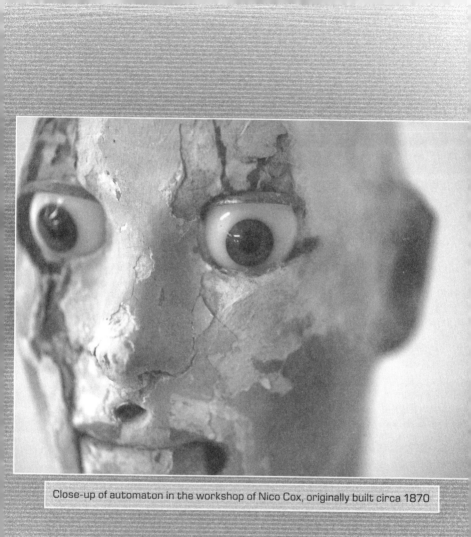

Close-up of automaton in the workshop of Nico Cox, originally built circa 1870

CHAPTER 2

In the (Uncanny)
Valley of the Dolls

n an enormous Goodwill in Seattle, Washington, the horologist Brittany "Nico" Cox and I sorted through a sad and somewhat creepy assortment of discarded and possibly once-loved dolls hoping to find one with large, realistic glass eyes. We talked about how we were both a little mortified at the thought of having to smash a porcelain head to extract the eyes, but were determined to get just the right ones for our deeply sacred task. I had come to Seattle in the hopes of learning something about the supernatural roots of artificial life, and in the days spent in Nico's studio in the Columbia City neighborhood, I probed the possibility that we might make a simple automaton. I had given up on my endeavor to build a golem, the magical creation of Jewish legend, but wasn't ready to abandon the spirit of that quest. I found it again in these wonderful mechanical objects that have their origins in our mythic consciousness, when magic and mechanics were believed to be part of the same natural principles.

To understand this urge to reach out to the divine by means of human handiwork, I had to get as close as I could to the techniques and craft people used and believed made this possible. The automata and other artificial constructs that are imbued with living attributes are, I believe, one of the earliest forms of this effort. There is speculation that even the earliest cave paintings were a way of conjuring the soul or power of the animals depicted—the mere crafting of a symbolic image enough to tap into a form of magic. Indeed, representation and symbolic thinking are a critical early step of human infant development, a philosophical and neurological recapitulation of our cultural heritage. And what could be a more perfect representation of our own inherent divinity than the creation of life—without sexual union. Nevertheless, it still took the best efforts of a man and a woman together, but here they were sorting through old dolls in a Goodwill.

Unfortunately, none of the dolls had the eyes we needed. Most were either too small or ridiculously large like Japanese anime characters. There was something lifelike about all of them, though, and their haunted quality would take hold of me for the time Nico and I were together. While I dug through the boxes of dolls, Nico phoned a friend who has a shop for taxidermists to see if he had any glass eyes, but his were only for animals. Our last effort found us in Archie McPhee, a Seattle novelty shop that sells a huge assortment of strange and unique objects: rubber chickens, masks, plastic animals, gag gifts. On a shelf at the far end of the store, we discovered a box of dozens of eyes in assorted sizes made from a dark, hazy glass. After much sorting and searching, we found three sets of eyes that had the personality we were after: not quite lifelike, but having the quality of, dare I say it, a soul. There was also something sad and disquieting about them. Life seemed possible within them, even though I knew rationally they were just pieces of colored glass.

On the drive back to her workshop, I asked Nico—one of the few and foremost horologists who repairs and restores antique automata—what she understands about this impulse to create life, or the semblance of life, and why it also threatens our sense of stability. For her, it presents itself as a series of questions: "What are the creative capacities in human beings versus God? What is it to be a part of a spiritual realm?" She explained, "If we can imagine it, can we create it? What are our creative and cognitive capacities as humans compared to a divine creator?"

While Christianity posits that the imitation of God—*imitatio dei*—is to model one's moral behavior, the eighteenth-century political philosopher and deist Thomas Paine proposed an extension of what it means to be like the creator: "The true Deist has but one Deity, and his religion consists in contemplating the power, wisdom, and benignity of the Deity in his works, and in endeavoring to imitate him in everything moral, scientifical, and mechanical." Paine was inspired by Isaac Newton, who had argued that the universe could be imagined as a great celestial clock, each part influencing the other as gears in the works. Indeed, the contemporary theologian and historian Alister E. McGrath posits that it was the cathedral clock of Strasbourg that was "singled out as a worthy analogue of the celestial machine." There were three versions of the astronomical clock, the first having been completed in 1354. The second version of the clock, working during Newton's lifetime, showed the movements of the planets and both lunar and solar eclipses, and was decorated with automata performing certain routines, including chariots representing the days of the week, a figure of Jesus performing benediction, and of course the requisite skeleton representing death and mortality.

This clockwork universe would also function as a metaphor that extends to God as the clockmaker, the timeless creator whose precision works cannot only be seen in the heavens, but in the very forms of nature, in the animal kingdom, and in the human body itself. Religious thinkers, however, fought to make sure the soul—and its accompanying moral obligations—did not get lost in the workings of God's great clock. In 1802, the theologian William Paley amplified what had come to be known as the "watchmaker analogy." Paley describes himself walking along a garden lane and coming across a watch in the grass. It's easy to deduce that the watch didn't grow out of the ground, Paley reflects. Something this complicated must have had a maker. Paley then goes on to look at the world around him: ants crawling with purpose, ancient trees rising toward the heavens, the sun warming the earth. How could these things, so much more complex than even a watch, not have had an intelligent maker also? In Paley's vision, God surely made the universe, but he did not abandon it. It continues because he wills it, Paley notes. And God wills it because he loves the world.

With the increase of a scientific worldview, thinkers like Paine still believed there was a secret order to the universe, but one of a great machine, a clock, created by God like the clockmaker at his bench. Paine and other deists could not make Paley's leap of faith. God had indeed made the world, but he took no interest in it, did not intervene on behalf of his creatures, and certainly did not act in history. Like a watch, God wound and set the universe on its way. But the human being, too, can become a creator, using essentially the same blueprint. Creating doesn't invoke any supernatural agency, but the notion of the clockmaker God animated an activity like mechanics and other human technological endeavors. The automaton would prove to be a worrisome example, however, of our ability to craft models of God's universe.

Nico's work with automata began in just the right sort of way, with a bachelor's degree in metaphysics and epistemology from the University of Texas. She wanted to explore how early forms of artificial intelligence were both asking metaphysical questions as well as challenging metaphysical ideas. Nico understood that these questions were better posed in a tangible way, and to work with those objects that first posed such questions. An automaton known as the Silver Swan led her to what would become her life's work. Built by James Cox in 1773, the life-sized swan was designed and engineered by the inventor John Joseph Merlin. Nico told me about the swan over dinner at an Ethiopian restaurant, glass eyes still in their paper bag on the seat next to me like incubating lives. She described a living thing born out of the artificial. But I wondered which aspect of it was the most essential, the clockwork or the shadow of the real. "They used real swans as models and even created replica feathers," Nico said. The details in the feathers were hand-carved and engraved, a method known as chasing. "Each single one," Nico explained. "And the swan is covered in hundreds." Its neck is made of over one hundred thirteen connected rings that freely move "like a Slinky, but each one nests inside of the other." Fusee chains, which Nico described are like a bike chain, increase and decrease the tension in the neck so that the swan can dip its head into the "pond" and eat a fish. Nico's eyes brightened. "It actually gobbles up a little fish. It sees it and eats it."

The swan is currently housed in Bowes Museum in Barnard Castle in England. "When people look at it and experience it, it comes across as a vulnerable being. It's so delicate; it has a life of its own." At the International Exposition in Paris in 1867, Mark Twain saw the swan and later wrote that it "had a living grace about his movements and a living intelligence in his eyes." Twain's sentimental view of the swan exposes a concern that mechanical objects—specifically automata—might have a soul, a spirit that is essential to its function. It's here that I first began to see that the very idea of life, of creation, is deeply bound up in the process of making and inventing. As Nico told me, one of her mentors, Matthew Read, had worked on the now-antique swan and had an affinity and an affection for it such that he could never have for a simple clock. Although Nico describes Read as the epitome of the dry Englishman, it's easy to imagine he saw the swan as a delicate life that needed to be nurtured, a creature he wanted to heal, like a parent at the bed of a sick child. The swan was so damaged by previous caretakers that Read's task seemed almost impossible. "Every time this thing operated," Nico said, "it was tearing itself apart." Read needed to figure out which parts were later replaced and how they were affecting the original components. Nico fell in love. The swan was a life that needed tending.

Nico's path from the University of Texas to the swan automaton was a long one. First there was watchmaking school in Seattle, where she learned how to build a watch and fabricate various parts. From there she went to West Dean College in the United Kingdom, where she specialized in clocks and related dynamic objects and learned how to make every gear, pinion, and hand. She then received a postgraduate degree certified through the University of Sussex in conservation of clocks and related dynamic objects, and where she received her master's. But all she really wanted was to work with automata.

Nico's studio was nestled between a hair salon and an Ethiopian restaurant; the shabby storefront didn't offer any clue as to what was inside. Not unlike Dr. Who's TARDIS, the interior appeared much bigger than one would imagine looking at it from the street. In fact, nothing inside was suggested by the slowly gentrifying urban neighborhood in which it sits. Nico's workshop was a deeply artful protest against the modernity bumping against her door. The first floor was crowded with machines, some of which were familiar to me, like lathes and drills, but most I could not identify. Nico walked me around, pointing them out: straight-line machine, rose engine, pinion cutter, gear cutting machine, fly press, draw bench. There was a dial printing machine and a spotting machine. A Leonard lap and a Hauser jig borer. Two drill presses. A rolling mill. But what I heard was "alembic, retort, crucible, athanor," the alchemical tools used to perform what was called the Great Work, the spiritual exertion of the will over the material world.

Upstairs is where the more intricate and hand-done work is performed. What makes Nico unique among people who work with and restore automata is that she can do all the things museums require many individual craftspeople to do. Here were various benches with hand tools, small drills, bookshelves, and of course, Nico's current automata repair jobs. No matter their size, there is a delicacy and vague melancholia dwelling in these objects as if they know they are incongruous with the world. Nico brought me over to a small workbench where she picked up and wound a small silver box by inserting a key. From the top, a little round door flipped open, out of which emerged a tiny bird that began to sing and flap its wings. Under a small bell jar is a similar unboxed bird that Nico is repairing. In a cabinet nearby, Nico showed me drawer after drawer of antique bird feathers she uses to restore these kinds of automata. She also presented the mechanism for one that was under repair, a compact clockwork movement with the addition of a tiny set of bellows that compresses air through a small whistle. A set of cams works to adjust the bellows to produce the birdsong. All this miniaturization and precision craftsmanship in order to produce a model of life astonished me. What was even more startling was seeing the mechanics of how the bird box functioned, and yet how readily I suspended my disbelief when Nico wound it up and the little singing bird emerged. The quality of being remained.

Walking around the room we stopped at a large doll in the figure of a black banjo player. It needed serious repair, and Nico had been working on every part of it, from its clothing to its movement. It was originally manufactured by the French company Phalibois sometime between 1870 and 1900. The automaton needed to be entirely rebuilt. When Nico received it, it had badly damaged legs and torso and an earlier amateur repair job had injured it further. The eyelids and mouth were split where they joined to the head. Nico outsourced a doll clothing restorer to remake the clothing and an instrument maker to repair the damage to the banjo and strings. Nico's own work was concentrated on the mechanism itself, which she'd had to completely overhaul, but was now working well enough that she could show me its basic functions. The automaton strums its banjo while a hidden music box plays a lilting lullaby. The musician's eyes begin to slowly close until it falls asleep, and then after a few long seconds it abruptly wakes up and begins to play again. When fully restored, the automaton has a working cam and wire mechanism that cause its chest to rise and fall. Even without its clothes and the visible works, it was still enchanting, and maybe more so because of what was lacking, what was exposed. Stripped of the extra layers of artifice, the automaton in its raw state highlighted the sense of eeriness, this somewhat broken thing instilling a familiar sense of sadness and lost history, like an elderly person on their deathbed that inspires both pity and fear.

But there is also the unique quality that comes about when the mechanism is completely hidden from view and the function is mysterious. It's this response that Nico hopes to elicit, a sensation she believes can't be produced by anything else other than automata: "This is a feeling that I think is experienced by everyone when they see an automaton, especially when they're surprised by it." Nico described the illusion of the automata being something more than what is immediately apparent. The mechanism for the tiny bird is obviously contained in the box, but it also seems impossible something so complex could be hidden. Moreover, when the bird pops out and begins its routine, nothing about it suggests it's connected to a complex set of works. The mechanism of all these objects is essentially the same. A spring provides the energy, a gear train transmits the energy, and cams dictate the motion and movement of the automaton. The challenge in building and restoring an automaton is how to make the purely mechanical appear lifelike. As Nico explained, it's a balance of "getting all the mechanical properties that have to there to produce the minimum illusion, but then fleshing out the details that help it suggest the feeling."

Automata—as well as any other technology that allows for the supernatural to manifest in the world—give rise to the true meaning of the word "occult": concealed. It is the potential exposure that elicits the feelings of dread. This anxiety is typically rooted in the belief that what is being revealed should remain hidden—at risk of death or, in the least, heresy. The automaton becomes a form of magic, a tool that disrupts the normal course of things and parts the curtain between the worlds. The persistent idea that through some form of arcane methods human beings can imitate the most potent of God's attributes is an ancient one, a hope and fear that our ability to create life from nothingness would thereby ensure our immortality.

The history of artificial life is one that reveals our suspicions and fears about our creative capacities, and the automaton is caught between the poles of virtuous human ingenuity and the dangerous invocation of infernal powers. It's an old, old fear, one that extends back to the origins of monotheism. The possibility that the demonic or other ungodly powers are what fuel artificial life is partly what drives the prohibition against graven images found in the Hebrew Bible as well as the destruction of Catholic statues—even those of Jesus and the saints—during the Protestant Reformation. For the ancient Israelites, the threat came from the worship of other gods in the form of statues and idols. These objects—built by human beings—were often believed to be the vessels through which the gods spoke. In Judaism, whose deity cannot even be seen by Moses, this fear of graven images is at the heart of the religious identity. Nevertheless, the instinct to give form and shape to the divine is unrelenting as in the story of Exodus when the ancient Israelites pleaded with Moses's brother, Aaron, to show them what their all-powerful desert god looked like. Aaron has them melt down all their gold and he forms it into the shape of a calf—a common animal form for the gods of the surrounding tribes. Moses, on his way to bring his people the Ten Commandments, is, of course, furious. He smashes the tablets, destroys the calf, and makes the Israelites drink its powdered form.

Other cultures' mythology offers several tales about statues and other living constructs. The ancient Greek epic poem *The Argonautica* tells of the bronze statue Talus, the protector of Crete. Talus was built by the god Hephaestus, an artificer of other wonders, including singing maidens known as *celedones* and horses that breathed fire. But Talus was constructed with a fatal flaw, an organic vein that ran from his foot to his neck. This thin vulnerability would, of course, be his undoing when "he grazed his ankle on a pointed crag; and the ichor gushed forth like melted lead."

Called Vulcan by the Romans, Hephaestus was the god of blacksmiths and volcanoes, sculpture and fire. Like many myths, the creation of human beings in Greek mythology involves mud and the breath of life, a note-for-note similarity with the story of Adam's creation in Genesis. It was fire, however, that the titan Prometheus stole from Zeus and gave to humanity so they could invent and build. This is Hephaestus's tool, the method by which his marvelous constructions were made. Fire is the activating agent for the artificial, unlike air, which gives life to human beings. (It is notable that the golem is given life via breath as opposed to fire, which is what powered the forge of Hephaestus to create artificial life.)

Fire, by way of lightning, became the metaphor for electricity in the story of the most famed artificial creature, Mary Shelley's novel *Frankenstein*. The books and films it inspired tend to reduce the fear of creating artificial life as that of the conceit of playing God. The novel's original subtitle, *The Modern Prometheus*, is, of course, a direct reference to the Greek myth Prometheus. But Prometheus is not playing God. He is offering the world power—thought to belong only to the divine—to create its own destiny. It is not only Greek myths that inspired Shelley's novel, though. There is speculation that Grimm's telling of the golem (as described earlier) was another likely source for Shelley.

Frankenstein is also the location where the golem becomes technology, rather than a religious or magical device. Victor Frankenstein is merely using science in place of the divine power. Frankenstein does not want to be God; his desire is to perfect what God has already made. Frankenstein is attempting to defy mortality, to conquer death. Therefore, electricity (fire) and not breath is what brings the misshapen creature to life. The dread at Frankenstein's creation is caused not only by the sense that a human being is playing God, but also by the understanding that the monster itself reveals God's secret workings of the universe, workings that should stay veiled. Spiritual crafting becomes human ingenuity.

Nevertheless, in the ability to create artificial life either from piecing together parts of the dead or building a construct from clay or mechanical parts, the imitation of a divine process is still inherent in the act. To make life when there wasn't life before has long been believed to be the purview of God. And even God has claimed this feat as the best representation of power. When Job questions God's unjust tampering with his life, God responds:

> *Look at Behemoth,*
> *which I made just as I made you;*
> *it eats grass like an ox.*
> *Its strength is in its loins,*
> *and its power in the muscles of its belly.*
> *It makes its tail stiff like a cedar;*
> *the sinews of its thighs are knit together.*
> *Its bones are tubes of bronze,*
> *its limbs like bars of iron.*

The prohibition against graven image would be softened over time, particularly regarding simply drawing and carving the likeness of animals, and eventually the Roman love of sculpture and other plastic arts would influence the Christian empire with innumerable statues of saints, the Virgin Mary, and Jesus. This would extend even into Church-sanctioned automata, including a mechanical Christ whose eyes and mouth moved, devils that the historian Jessica Riskin refers to as "Satan-machines," which "howled and stuck out their tongues," and, of course, the fantastic astronomical clock mentioned earlier.

In gardens and grottoes of the Renaissance, moving statues became toys of the wealthy and would capture the popular imagination. The once-famed Hortus Palatinus garden, designed by the architect Inigo Jones, contained numerous wonders built by the engineer Salamon de Caus, including mechanical birds and water-powered organs using complicated pneumatics that elevated it to what the historian Frances Yates calls a "magical atmosphere." Other automata built by de Caus include a cyclops that plays a pan flute, the god Dionysus drinking from a wine cask, and a scene of the hero Perseus killing a dragon.

Automata like these inspired the inclusion of magically constructed automata in many literary works of the time, including an animated brass horse in *The Canterbury Tales* and the living statue in the likeness of the deceased Hermione in Shakespeare's *The Winter's Tale*, which could be depicted onstage, creating the illusion of a statue coming to life for the audience.

Animating living statues was believed to be a sorcerous act, but this power also demonstrated the magician's ability to connect to the divine, drawing down heavenly powers to create wonders. Renaissance mages looked to the ancient world and other lands for knowledge of these miracles. The magic of animating statues is astrological in nature, requiring the planetary spirits to descend into the material forms and animate them, often in the form of speech. One of the earliest examples is found in the *Corpus Hermeticum*, a collection of texts from the second century, first translated from Greek into Latin by the priest and astrologer Marsilio Ficino in 1464, and then believed by scholars and theologians to have been written much earlier by Hermes Trismegistus, an Egyptian priest who possessed preternatural divine wisdom. In the text known as "To Asclepius," Hermes and his student Asclepius discuss "statues, ensouled with sense, and filled with spirit, which work such mighty and such strange results, statues which can foresee what is to come, and which perchance can prophesy, foretelling things by dreams and many other ways." The *Corpus* would form the basis for the magical tradition of the Renaissance, and the possibility that an artificial construct could be imbued with something like prophetic speech cracked open the imagination.

As the historian Minsoo Kang makes clear, magic could be either divine or demonic depending on the source of the power the magician employed. Eventually, magic becomes compartmentalized into either natural magic "through which one could perform marvelous acts" or the magic that requires conjuring demons or other spirits, often called necromancy, the blackest of all arts. If an automaton was thought to be powered by a spirit, it was far more suspect than one that was constructed using natural magic. A master craftsman using special knowledge of God's creation would decree an automaton marvelous, a wonder to behold. The same object thought to be powered by a demonic entity called forth by a necromancer would render it unholy and blasphemous.

It was René Descartes in the seventeenth century who resolved this tension by proposing that the human is also a clockwork mechanism, possessed of a spirit—the ghost in the machine—that was imbued with reason and will by God. Thus, who was to say that we could not create a mechanism with the same component parts? This idea would result in an explosion of automata, including a chess player, a fortune-telling magician, a flautist, and even a duck that ate a bit of food and excreted it. Descartes's machine man shifted the ambivalent nature of the automaton away from superstitions about magic and toward more complicated questions about our own inherent divinity. Do we still hold a special place in God's creation if we are merely nothing more than automata that can be simulated so easily by gears and bellows?

The more rational understanding of the human being as a perfectly constructed machine and a belief its functions could be replicated with clockwork didn't assuage the deep-seated worry that automata were controlled by supernatural forces. In the 1816 story "The Sandman" by E. T. A. Hoffmann, we meet the sensitive Nathanael, who never quite got over the terror of seeing his father killed in a strange alchemical accident. Throughout his life, the character is haunted by the figure of the man who was his father's assistant, Coppelius, described as "loathsome and repulsive" with "huge, gnarled, hairy hands," and once caught the young Nathanael spying on them during one of their experiments. Nathanael overheard the two men working toward the peak effort of their labors, which called for the creation of a set of eyes. An experiment days later resulted in the explosion that killed Nathanael's father. Years later an anxious Nathanael meets a barometer and eyeglass salesman named Coppola, who he believes is a doppelgänger of Coppelius. He also begins to take classes with a professor of physics named Spalazani and soon falls in love with his daughter Olympia, whose eyes he notices are at first lifeless, but begin to become "inflamed with ever-increasing life." Olympia is described as having a "beautifully shaped face and figure," but people also notice there is "something stiff and measured about her walk." Olympia can sing and play the piano with great skill, but when Nathanael tries to speak with her, she only ever says, "Ah, ah!" One day Nathanael decides to ask Olympia to marry him and when he arrives at her home he hears a terrible commotion. Inside, Coppola is wrestling with Spalazani over Olympia, pulling at her limbs, their voices arguing about eyes and clockwork. Coppola flees with

Olympia, now a "lifeless" doll, leaving on the floor a pair of eyes. Nathanael never recovers from the horror, feeling forever haunted by Coppola/Coppelius, and eventually throws himself from a tower. The doll is an artificial construct, made possible by a terrible mix of magic and technology. Its very existence—and its inability to truly love—sow the seeds of Nathanael's suicide.

Poor Nathanael might be an exaggeration to serve the narrative, but the origin of his despair was one that mirrored how the automaton existed in the imagination: an artificial construct that appears perfectly lifelike, but lacking an essential quality—a soul. In his brief 1919 essay, "The Uncanny," Freud uses "The Sandman" to explore the unsettling feeling when confronted with a fissure in our day-to-day experience, a moment that feels both real and unreal at the same time. As an example, he offers the idea of "the double," such as an inanimate object that has the qualities of life or a living thing that takes on a characteristic of being a simulacrum. It is unnerving, and sometimes can even elicit a sense of what the theologian Rudolf Otto calls the *mysterium tremendum*, a sense of being in the presence of the noumenal, the demonic.

During the period "The Sandman" was written, automata were well known around Europe—particularly those known as The Draftsman, The Musician, and The Writer, built in the 1770s by the Swiss clockmaker Pierre Jaquet-Droz and his son Henri-Louis, with help from their friend and business partner Jean-Frédéric Leschot. The automata are incredibly lifelike, their movements graceful and smooth, and they can perform incredibly complicated activities without an external gear assembly. They are completely self-contained, and so can be easily transported and displayed. The Draftsman, a young boy dressed in red velvet and lace, sits at a desk, where he draws either a dog, a butterfly, or a portrait of Marie Antoinette or Louis XVI. The Draftsman looks concentratedly at his work, and will even blow away dust from the drawing as he draws. The Writer, the automaton that inspired the 2007 young adult illustrated novel *The Invention of Hugo Cabret*, is also in the likeness of a young boy at a desk. It can write forty characters long after first dipping its quill into an ink stand and tapping off the excess. The messages were essentially programmed by a series of cam wheels installed vertically in its back that could be set to various positions. Their sister, The Musician, plays a small harpsichord. Her eyes follow her hands, and her chest rises and falls with her breath.

At this time, the place of the automaton in the human imagination was both one of fascination and deep suspicion, but it's difficult to know exactly how far people's mistrust went. Harry Houdini recounts the story of Henri-Louis exhibiting the automata in Spain, where the machines were advertised as being powered by supernatural forces. Houdini claims Henri-Louis was jailed by the Inquisition, his inventions seen as heretical. He was eventually released, but the Inquisition kept the automata, and it is said they put one automaton on trial to coax out a confession that it and the others were indeed demonic devices. It was, of course, unable to answer their questions about whether or not it was a pawn of the devil. Later historians would correct some of these details. The trip to Spain was years before the construction of the three famed automata, and it was actually Pierre who went, bringing with him an automaton in the likeness of a shepherd and his dog, specifically to show King Ferdinand VI and his court. During the demonstration, Ferdinand reaches toward the dog, which elicits a bark at the king, frightening many of the people in attendance. Later, one of the king's ministers asks the automaton the time, and—the story goes—it responds. The atmosphere in the room was now tense, and Pierre, thinking he might be arrested for witchcraft, offers to demonstrate to the Grand Inquisitor how the machines truly function, keeping his life and his head intact.

People were also becoming more familiar with clocks, some with incredibly complicated mechanisms that included calendar and alarm features, but the automaton with its imitation of life still evoked feelings of wonder and fear in equal measure. Moreover, the image of the mechanical or artificial man on trial would also remain part of our long spiritual fear of machines imitating human beings, potentially replacing us entirely. The 1935 film *Bride of Frankenstein* involves a scene of the creature strapped to a chair, waiting to be tried, and decades later, the android Data—one of the most popular characters in the Star Trek franchise—would defend his right to live independently, claiming some aspect of a soul.

With our glass eyes, we set out to build a simple automaton in Nico's studio. My earlier effort to make a golem was more like trying to learn a complex grammar, but now I found myself building something. Perhaps they are the same thing. The golem is made from a magical procedure, but its nature as a construct invokes the very essence of that strange etymological relationship between the words "magic" and "technology," where magic is another means to craft an intent into a material form. The original Greek term "magic" is the compound word *magikē-tekhnē* or "the art of the magician." And if, as Rabbi Riess told me, the true golem is the spiritual man I make inside myself, then technology is not merely an external experience, but the inner process of making that moves through all things. In this view, human creation will always be a mirror, albeit at a microcosmic scale, of divine creation. Moreover, when we build, we participate in furthering creation.

Our little automaton becomes another extension of ourselves in the world and reminds us of our own miraculous inner workings.

Nico found a small piece of wood, about six square inches and one-eighth-inch thick. We drilled out holes for the eyes and glued them in on one side so they faced out the other. Nico wanted to emphasize not only the mechanical function of eyes opening and closing, but the quality of life. She cut two small pieces of leather from some scrap in the shape of eyelids, and we glued them on. On the other side of the wood, we constructed a simple mechanism using springs and thread so that when a string was pulled below the device, the eyelids would slowly close and then open when the string was released.

As we labored, the automaton began to resolve into something that looked both curiously alive and artificial. I could see what was artifice. Even though I had worked with Nico to build it, had come to understand the principles of simple machines that produced the desired effect, there still arose a quality of *being* that was undeniable. Partly this was imposed on the little figure by my expectation. But it was also because I had entered into a kind of craft, even as a mostly unhelpful assistant to Nico's handiwork, that stretches back centuries. Making, as an activity, was not simply about the construction of our little automaton. We were fashioning it with our hands, with pieces of things cut, drilled, bent, glued, and repurposed, and, as Thomas Paine remarked, imitating God's creative capacity. The uncanny still crept in, however: an unfinished face with two strange eyes staring out sleepily from soft leather lids.

Handling the materials and manipulating them toward a magical intent—in this case the creation of life, or the semblance thereof—clarified for me that the key to the relationship between technology and the supernatural is how the human element has inserted itself through hacking both materials and the imagination. The history of the automaton is one where a rational understanding of the natural world and mechanical technology conspire with the imagination to produce feelings of supernatural and magical significance. These feelings are not illusory or false. They arise out of an imperative to link our handiwork to the divine, to ensure that as technology seems to drive us further away from spiritual and magical realities that we rebel—we *hack*—by turning our devices and machines into methods of recovering what may be lost. I had built a little contraption that contained within it this profound historical quest, but it only referenced the supernatural via all its deep associations. The otherworldly was an idea inserted into the various techniques. My exploration would next take me to when magic and technology were indistinct from each other, and where performance, technology, and illusion can become so indistinguishable from the supernatural reality they seek to disclose.

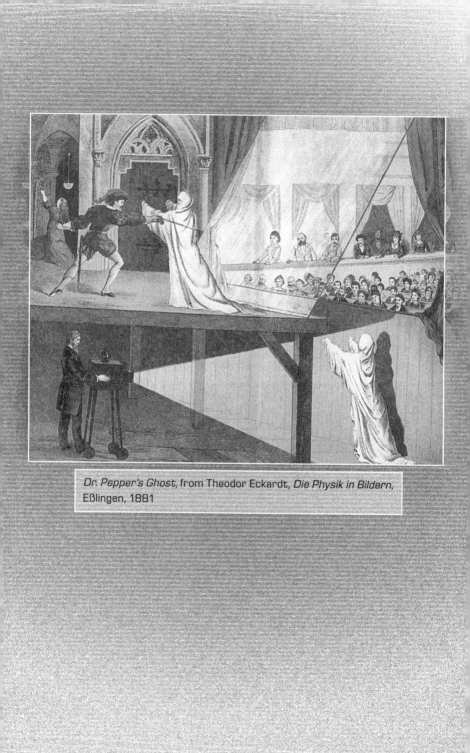

Dr. Pepper's Ghost, from Theodor Eckardt, *Die Physik in Bildern*, Eßlingen, 1881

CHAPTER 3

Rough Magic

During a recent performance of William Shakespeare's *The Tempest* at the American Repertory Theater (ART) in Cambridge, Massachusetts, produced and directed by Raymond Teller (of Penn & Teller), I found myself looking straight into the heart of magic. The enchanter Prospero, marooned on an island, is attempting to undo the dissolution of his family and restore his and his daughter Miranda's place by using all the arcane forces at his disposal, including the trickster spirit Ariel, indebted to the magician who released him from imprisonment in a tree. Ariel himself is a master sorcerer, capable of feats of wonder, and is the source of most of the magic that occurs in the play. In one scene, Prospero places Ariel in a box with only Ariel's head and legs exposed to both remind him of his own power and of Ariel's once having been a slave to the witch Sycorax, who kept him captive, "Into a cloven pine; within which rift/Imprison'd thou didst painfully remain." Prospero magically begins to twist Ariel's head around and around, a classic stage magic effect that suddenly feels ominous and preternatural seeing it within the narrative of the play.

Ariel, played by the actor and magician Nate Dendy, employs "real" magic, completely erasing the line between magic as performance and the occult magic of Prospero. Ariel's magic is supernatural, expressed onstage using sleight of hand techniques and technology that, as Nate explained to me over a video call, was not any more advanced than was available to the Elizabethan-era production when the play was first staged. In Act III, Scene III of *The Tempest*, a miraculous banquet is brought onstage by "strange shapes," and later Ariel appears to magically whisk the feast away. Shakespeare's stage direction calls for Ariel to "[clap] his wings upon the table" and then "with a quaint device, the banquet vanishes." "Quaint" here does not mean charming or picturesque as we tend to use the word today. "Quaint" for Shakespeare meant ingenious and cunningly devised. In other words, technology. In the case of the banquet table, Shakespeare likely employed a trapdoor that disappeared the table from view. Nate would not, of course, tell me the secrets of the ART's staging of the play, but offered this: "Our supply shop is places like Michael's and Home Depot. We use the stuff anyone can get, we just use it in ways you can't possibly think of."

The use of real stage magic in *The Tempest* also calls to mind the earliest ideas of how theater should function. The Greek plays involving Dionysus were meant to be initiatory. Edith Hall, a classicist and historian at King's College London, explains that just as the characters are seen to be in thrall to the god's madness—akin to a state of altered consciousness—the audience is asked to imagine that experience for themselves. She writes, "Drama demands that performer and spectator collude in a suspension of the empirically 'real' world, and an involvement in a world that is not really there." Teller's codirector for *The*

Tempest, Aaron Posner, echoed this idea in an interview with the periodical *American Theater*, explaining that Teller's magic techniques have "the capacity to put the audience in the same mental place as the character—baffled, confused, surprised, horrified." As Nate explained it to me, this staging of *The Tempest* echoes this original idea of theater. The illusion of magic is necessary for the drama to be real for the audience: "Stage magic is being used as a storytelling device to bring you closer to what the characters are thinking and feeling and experiencing."

Beyond the theater, the gods of ancient Greece still enjoyed their temples, however, and so their houses became locations where technology was employed for ritual and religious purposes. The first-century engineer and inventor Hero of Alexandra designed divine marvels for the temples to cast a religious spell on the worshippers. Possibly by the patronage of priests, Hero's facility with mechanics and physics would have been used to create illusions of divine power in the temples. Hero designed dancing figures, slowly spinning statues powered by steam, and temple doors that opened by themselves, or rather, by the power of the gods. Hero even devised a portable temple, a tall pedestal with a stage on which the story of the god Dionysus was played out. This merging of performance, theatrics, and religion is at the heart of the origin of theater. The use of technology to demonstrate the workings of magic was not necessarily trickery, even though the intent was to impress a kind of spiritual wonder on the observer. As we saw, magic was understood to be a form of *techne*, or "craft," which included, according to Plato, geometry, sculpture, blacksmithing, and even prophecy. The philosopher Larry Hickman explains that magic, "like other forms of *techne*, involves the use of tools and artifacts according to a method to achieve certain desired results," but that magic, unlike technology, has a "gnostic core." Technology is essentially trying to solve a real-world problem by imposing a human-engineered solution. Magic is an attempt to solve a human problem using a spiritually engineered solution. In the heart of the temple, there is no longer this distinction.

Teller and Posner were also trying to erase this distinction onstage at the ART. When Ariel's supernatural feats are not merely alluded to but performed, the profound relationship between the occult and ritual transpires before us onstage. Indeed, the most potent magic is performance. Whether initiated by the shaman, witch, or magician in a chalk-drawn circle, it is in the performative moment that our consciousness is altered. Theater was the original means by which communities could be initiated into such mysteries without having to participate in the rituals themselves, other than as observers of the production. Yet this was and is not a passive experience; it is participatory because the audience bears witness, comprising the critical fourth wall of the mutual structure of the dream made real. Furthermore, the masks of the actor, a representation of the god that allows the deity to descend onto the stage, face the audience, without whom nothing would be perceived. Using stage magic to represent the occult magic demonstrated in the play is merely literalizing the method by which the occult already functions.

Reginald Scot had already published his infamous *Discoverie of Witchcraft* some thirty years earlier in 1584 by the time Shakespeare penned *The Tempest* circa 1610. Scot was a skeptical believer, a devout Christian who supposed witches were either falsely accused or mentally unstable women, and those who professed to have occult powers were master illusionists who duped the poor and the needy. Its sin was in its falsehood, but not due to any demonic origin. Scot reveals the methods employed by "charlatans" to dissuade people from believing in witches and the supernatural. But Scot was also a member of a small Christian order called the Family of Love, an Anabaptist sect deeply opposed to Catholicism, the denomination that constructed Notre Dame, a church known for its flying buttresses intended to induce a dizzying religious dread. While differing in magnitude, this is not unlike how a magician might use a charm or other illusion to convince someone they have been healed. It's no surprise, then, that Scot would find any attempt to artificially sway belief as suspect and un-Christian.

The Discoverie provides details on how conjurers and others claiming to have occult powers could deceive their marks. The use of lenses and other kinds of glass, such as crystals and prisms, can produce wondrous effects such as when "one man may see another man's image and not his own," or viewing things that are far away up close and vice versa. Scot also provides drawings for various methods of magical deception, such as a knife with a U-shaped indention in the blade, which can be used to create the illusion it has pierced the tongue or other body part. Scot does concur, however, that nature contains occult secrets that can be uncovered, a practice at the time called "natural magic." For example, it was believed that by tying a wild bull to a fig tree, some property of the tree tamed the animal, or that certain stones removed from the bellies of birds could "assuage thirst" and "make a drunken man sober." The belief that natural magic was a legitimate and God-sanctioned discipline of study and practice would lead the way to material developments in science and technology, but for a time, alas, it continued to tread along occult paths.

Scot was not interested or sympathetic, however, that the occult's employment of deception had purpose integral to its function. Suspension of disbelief is required not only for stage magic. For the occult imagination to function at all, rational conditions must be let go.

Known as the "professor of secrets," Giambattista della Porta was a mid-sixteenth-century scholar, but was truly the storybook definition of a mage, practicing his art amongst the upper and royal classes and writing the definitive work on natural magic of the time, entitled *Magiae Naturalis* (*Natural Magick*). Prior to him in 1533, the German theologian Cornelius Agrippa published his opus *Of Occult Philosophy*, in which he describes how magic is the "stitching" together of natural philosophy, mathematics, and theology. Through the manipulation of the four elements (earth, air, water, fire) and their corresponding celestial and earthly counterparts, the magician can speak with angels, divine the future, but most important, reveal the hidden blueprint of God's creation.

Porta's magic centered around this idea of correspondences, the belief that every aspect of nature is a microcosm of the divine and contains properties that draw its own qualities from a cosmic arrangement of forces. For example, Porta writes because a "Dog and a Wolf are at great enmity," if one is bitten by a rabid dog, wearing wolf skin "assuages the swelling of the Humor." In his book, Porta makes a clear distinction between the devilish activity of the sorcerer who conjures "foul spirits" and the pursuit of the godly magician who understands mathematics and physics, but also astrology, herbalism, and the divine properties of stones and animals. Having facility with arts such as metallurgy, Porta could also work wonders that he understood to be manipulations of nature using magical means. In one demonstration, Porta made a piece of iron jump around on the top of a table by moving a lodestone below the iron on the underside of the wood. Porta understood the magician should not reveal his secrets, in order to create a sense of wonder. As he writes, "For he that knows the causes of a thing done, doth not so admire the doing it," a lesson stage magicians have long taken to heart.

As I was speaking with Nate over video chat, I could see a poster behind him of the stage magician Howard Thurston from 1915. The illustration showed the dark-haired Thurston in tux and tails staring deeply down at a skull he holds in his hands from whose eye sockets spirits and imps rise into the air. Little red devils crawl on the magician's arm and back. I asked Nate why stage magic was often marketed as supernatural, as the magician's power coming from having first conjured demons and ghosts to assist with his performance. Nate happily told me about the magician Samri Baldwin, who referred to himself as the "White Mahatma" and whose poster for one of his acts states in bold letters, "The world's greatest psychic sensation." A blindfolded woman sits on a chair while an angel flies out of a heavenly sunlit sky to whisper in her ear. At her feet dozens of little devil children are handing her pieces of paper with questions on them: Will I be rich? Will I be married? Where is my papa? Nate explained that in the act, Samri's assistant would indeed blindfold herself and would put on an affect suggesting that the answers were coming from a supernatural agency. It's a fairly standard act, but, as Nate described, "The poster definitely overpromises what it is, even though the act is exactly what is advertised. You don't see the devil children. They don't make an appearance." (A similar kind of advertising would be used to great effect in the 1960s comic book advertisements for sea monkeys, which showed playful mer-people frolicking in their undersea kingdom, but that when put into water were tepid tiny shrimp.) Nevertheless, people flocked to his shows eager to witness his phenomenal powers. One reporter, writing for the *Burlington Evening Gazette* in 1897, warned anyone who might be a criminal to stay away from the show, as "Mr. Baldwin will know it." Baldwin created an entire mystique around himself, claiming to have studied the occult sciences in India. "Magic exists and works only because of the unwilling suspension of disbelief," Nate explained. The art of magic is when the audience is meeting the magician halfway, and like those first acts of religious performance, "emotionally engaging with you in some capacity, unspoken or not."

This union of audience and performer in service to a supernatural effect is at the heart of the religion known as Spiritualism. But the first mediums were not working in front of a large audience on a stage. Their methods, Nate said, were crude and ugly. "These were designed for bereaved mothers, fathers, and spouses." These were people who didn't need convincing. They brought their willingness to give over to it the moment they entered the medium's parlor. I wouldn't want to claim that all mediums of this time were frauds or deliberately trying to deceive their clients. Spiritualism as a religious and spiritual belief system has its own internal integrity, drawing its tenants from Christian mysticism but offering what it calls a "universal religion" that extends beyond any one denomination.

The origins of modern Spiritualism might very well lie in two Hydesville, New York, girls' ability to crack their toe knuckles, producing sounds akin to a table being rapped. In 1848, siblings Margaretta and Kate Fox, known as the Fox sisters, were fourteen and eleven, respectively, when they first began to communicate with spirits by calling on them to knock on the walls in response to questions. Their parents enlisted the help of neighbors to try and assess the source of the noises, and together they became convinced the girls were acting as conduits to the spirit world. Things became stranger still when the sisters named their new friend, calling him Mr. Splitfoot, a sinister moniker, conjuring an image of the devil whose hindquarters were often thought to be those of a goat, cloven hoofs and all. To calm the attention in their neighborhood, the two girls went to live with their older sister, Leah, in Rochester, but word of their abilities quickly spread and soon they were filling halls to demonstrate the knocking of spirits. There was no indication interest would spread beyond Rochester until the self-described prophet Andrew Jackson Davis—a devout follower of the eighteenth-century Christian mystical teachings of Emanuel Swedenborg—heard about Margaretta and Kate and brought them to New York City. A religious movement was born as the sisters took their mediumship on tour.

It appears that the subsequent media attention, public scrutiny, and the desperate need of the bereaved began to take a toll on the young women. In 1888, the newspaper *New York World* paid Margaretta $1,500 to admit she and her sister were perpetrating a hoax at a public demonstration where she would reveal how they were able to create the sound of rapping. A reporter for the Ohio newspaper the *Defiance Daily Crescent* describes a nervous Margaretta standing onstage "before a wearied and unsympathetic audience," unable to speak. A small table was placed next to her. The reporter writes: "Removing her shoe, she placed her right foot upon this table. The entire house became breathlessly still and was rewarded by a number of little short, sharp raps—those mysterious sounds which have for more than thirty years frightened and bewildered hundreds of thousands of people in this country and Europe." Margaretta would later retract her confession that it was just a matter of cracking her toe knuckles, but the damage had been done. Spiritualism's public demonstrations retreated into the parlor and more private settings, but for the most part the movement had already grown and developed in such a way that its believers held firm. Spiritualism was too necessary as a spiritual path. It presented a relationship to the divine that was broad-minded, without dogma, hopeful, and liberating.

Spiritualism offered a religion that was more progressive with regard to women, sexual norms, and—as with many forms of occultism—a belief that the individual could have a role in their own spiritual destiny. Spiritualism was also experiential. While there were several occult and esoteric societies that offered nontraditional spiritual wisdom such as Theosophy and Rosicrucianism, none could provide direct and immediate access to the spirit world. The medium and the client didn't need ritual, dense Hermetic texts, or to possess any arcane knowledge. It was believed that mediums should train their minds to allow the spirits to properly guide them. As Drew Gilpin Faust pointed out in her book *The Republic of Suffering*, this fit well within a culture that was inspired by a scientific, rational way of thinking. The attraction was also one of pragmatism; as Faust writes, it "offered belief that seemed to rely on empirical evidence rather than revelation and faith." Even abolitionists found support for their views in Charles Darwin's writing and other rational perspectives.

The enormous death toll of the Civil War and the trauma of a conflict that had pitted family members against one another was a factor in the rise of Spiritualism (and would resurge again after World War I for the same terrible losses). The desperate need to reconcile, to forgive, or to simply hope for a better life beyond one that could have fashioned such a brutal struggle kept mediums busy. Faust also notes that one of the attractive qualities of mediums over the local minister is that Spiritualism could link the living and the dead. The Boston Spiritualist newspaper *Banner of Light*, Faust observes, offered communications from dead soldiers such as "Lieut. Grebble," who admitted in life he did not believe in Spiritualism, but having found a medium through which to speak, now sends his "appeal from the land of the shadows."

Spiritualism's dependence on the work of mediums made it subject to increasing scrutiny, the most famous of which came by way of Harry Houdini. Houdini first began investigating Spiritualism out of an honest desire to contact his deceased mother. In his book *A Magician Among the Spirits*, Houdini unapologetically admits to his belief in life after death and that we will be reunited with our loved ones in the world to come. His own desire to communicate with his mother was a genuine one. He writes: "I believe in a Hereafter and no greater blessing could be bestowed upon me than the opportunity, once again, to speak to my sainted Mother who awaits me with open arms to press me to her heart in welcome, just as she did when I entered this mundane sphere." What Houdini found, however, was medium after medium performing tricks, sometimes ingenious ones, that convinced many people they were in communication with supernatural forces. These deceptions were often simple pieces of technological wizardry, and Houdini had no misgivings in explaining exactly how they were enacted. Take, for example, the rapping phenomena that originated with the Fox sisters. Houdini discovered many mediums simply tapped their knees on the undersides of tables, or secured a piece of wood to their leg, hidden under a skirt, that was "rapped" against the table. But others employed more technical methods, such as a mechanical knocker concealed in the heel of a shoe that is electrically engaged by a wire moving up the medium's leg and powered by a hidden battery.

The supernatural effects in the production of *The Tempest*, Nate told me, were even cruder than the methods employed by the mediums Houdini exposed. Nate described some of his performance as Ariel as basically Scotch tape, misdirection, and suggestion, techniques Houdini acknowledged. These simple methods were used in conjunction with mechanical effects so that sounds produced by a little concealed device could be made to seem as if they were coming from another area in the room. There is nothing elaborate or sophisticated in either case. Technology for the medium or for the stage magician is part of a wider repertoire of tools, and often needs to be as simple as possible while still providing the desired effect. "It's messy, it's ugly, it's dirty," Nate admitted. "There's not a lot of sophistication in magic, period." Consider the wizard in the 1939 film *The Wizard of Oz*, who offers a delightful exaggeration of the medium at work in his attempt to convince Dorothy and residents of the Emerald City that his power is supernatural and not to be trifled with. When Toto the dog pulls back the curtain, we see a bumbling illusionist pulling levers and speaking into a microphone. "Pay no attention to that man behind the curtain!" he bellows as he frantically tries to resume the effect of his performance, even as they see he is a small old man. His devices are hacked and messy stuff. This is no arcane power he is wielding, it's a contraption that is hard to manage and control.

Situated perfectly between authentic spiritual experiences and purely performative trickery were Ira and William Davenport, known as the Davenport brothers, who performed elaborate séances onstage. The brothers would step into a cabinet where their hands and feet were bound, hiding instruments such as a guitar and a trumpet. The cabinet would be closed and almost immediately the sounds of the instruments could be heard. Rushing to open the cabinet to catch them, a spectator would find the brothers still bound and immobile in their chairs. The brothers often concluded their performances by claiming not to know where their strange powers came from. In an 1864 issue of the London weekly *Saturday Review*, the brothers are quoted as saying, "We do not assert that our experiments are attributable to spiritual agency. We cannot tell how they are produced. . . . We profess to exercise a power of the nature and extent of which we know nothing beyond the fact that we have it." Their marketing told another story. Posters for their act called what they did "séances" and stated that they worked with "invisible agencies." In June of 1865, the stage magician John Nevil Maskelyne put on a demonstration in which he revealed Ira and William's secret. The brothers were master escape artists and could easily and quietly release themselves from their bonds, even in total darkness, and then once freed were able to create whatever ghostly ruckus they chose. Once the séance was over, they would just as adeptly secure themselves.

Staging Spiritualism would become a cottage industry, and while many magicians hoped to debunk the work of mediums by showing how their tricks were plied, others enjoyed the uncertainty they sowed. The differences between the Spiritualist performer and the magician staking a claim against Spiritualism was not always clear, as Fred Nadis makes clear in his book *Wonder Shows*. Nadis notes the wonderful absurdity of the fact that mediums and magicians bought their props from the same supply catalogs. A brief look at the advertising posters of magicians during the nineteenth century shows a blatant use of supernatural imagery to describe the source of the arcane power being wielded onstage. The two practices fed off each other.

The line between performance and occult magic has always been shadowy. The ceremonial magician has long understood the importance of ritual activity for inducing the proper state of consciousness. Ritual costumes, movement in a sacred space (often within a magic circle), the delivery of "lines" in the form of invocations, and even the use of incense and candlelight, and sometimes most important, keeping your secrets.

In *Letters of a Russian Traveler, 1789–1790*, twenty-three-year-old Nikolay Mikhaïlovich Karamzin wrote of his journey through Europe. A Freemason, Karamzin was particularly interested in the esoteric and the occult, and it was in Germany that he learned the story of Johann Georg Schröpfer, another Freemason, but one who fancied himself a necromancer. Schröpfer owned a café in Leipzig where a number of Freemasons gathered. Schröpfer became interested in the fraternity, and later started his own lodge, where he claimed the true secrets of Freemasonry would be revealed, which for Schröpfer meant communicating with spirits.

According to the tale told to Karamzin's friend, an acquaintance of his went to see one of Schröpfer's séances, where he witnessed "a great number of guests who were continually being served punch," which was likely drugged. Schröpfer led the spectators into a sealed room covered with black cloth (which would be the decorative preference of mediums through the centuries), where he drew a magic circle on the ground. After a dramatic monologue imploring the spirits to appear as Schröpfer waved a sword in the air, "the spectators felt an electric shock, heard a clap of thunder, and saw above the credenza a thin vapor which gradually thickened, and finally assumed human form." It's clear that Schröpfer had some knowledge of ceremonial magic, using the forms and rituals for his demonstrations. The use of a sword to conjure spirits was a customary practice in many of the grimoires that would have been popular in his time. As a Freemason, Schröpfer likely recognized the value of pageantry and ritual to impress spiritual ideas and hoped to inject the traditional Masonic rites with occult flourishes. And while the sword might have been used simply for dramatic effect, there is indication that Schröpfer was becoming more and more convinced by his own performance.

Another tool or prop Schröpfer utilized was a magic lantern, an optical device whose invention is often ascribed to the astronomer Christiaan Huygens around 1659. The magic lantern works by illuminating a glass plate that is inserted horizontally between two lenses: the first focuses the light source (usually an oil lamp) onto the slide, and the other lens projects the image onto a wall or other surface. This, along with an instrument known as a glass harmonica (different-sized glass bowls attached to a spindle are touched with the musician's fingers) that produces otherworldly, spectral sounds, along with spiked punch, would have produced a great deception.

Schröpfer was popular at the time, and his shows became more and more elaborate until he found himself in debt. On October 8, 1774, while Schröpfer was walking with friends, he told them he was going to perform a necromantic feat unlike any of his ghostly conjurations. He ran ahead until they lost sight of him, only to find him farther up the path dead from a gunshot wound. There was no shooter to be found. Conspiracy theories rose around him, with Karamzin noting the conjecture that Schröpfer was working for Jesuits "who once more were trying to control the mind of men," and was assassinated.

In the late 1700s, Étienne-Gaspard Roberts hacked the magic lantern by placing his device on wheels. By moving the lantern smoothly back and forth, the images could be made to grow very quickly or disappear suddenly. Roberts mystified Paris with his performances, called "phantasmagoria," where he conjured devils, demons, ghosts, and other supernatural creatures, exploiting the spiritual concerns raised by our ability to peer into places once hidden, particularly with the invention of the microscope. Roberts also used smoke and sound effects, and like

Schröpfer could induce a state of altered consciousness in the audience, albeit without the spiked punch. In his memoirs, Roberts wrote that his intention was to demonstrate that spirits and devils were products of the imagination, made visible by scientific techniques, even as he opened his shows by working his audiences into a state of agitated excitement.

The phantasmagorias were held in the darkened crypt of an abandoned chapel, decorated "with black draperies and pictured with the emblems of mortality." Roberts would throw incense onto a dish of burning coals in the center of the room, creating a kind of hypnotic aura—not unlike Schröpfer's method. One spectator reported him then creating heightened expectation by announcing, "Citizens and gentlemen, I am not one of those adventurers and impudent swindlers who promise more than they can perform. I have assured the public in the *Journal de Paris* that I can bring the dead to life, and I shall do so." One man asked to see the spirit of his dead wife, and Roberts cast a spell by throwing assorted items onto the fire that symbolized aspects of their love, such as butterflies and sparrow feathers, which worked on the audience's own generative and magical thinking. A phantom suddenly appeared in the form of a woman, "with her bosom uncovered and her hair floating about her . . . and smiled on the young man with the most tender regard and sorrow." Rather than be comforted, the man was terrified, cried out, "Heavens! It's my wife come to life again," and quickly fled the theater. If the man had stayed to the end, he would have watched as Roberts explained that his conjured spirits were created with "optical science" and that these were the same techniques that magicians of the ancient world used as well. This was still not enough to persuade those already convinced that real spirits had joined them in the crypt.

The phantasmagoria show would reenter the public consciousness by way of a contrivance known as Pepper's Ghost. The United States patent #221,605, titled "Improvement in apparatus for producing optical illusions" and registered on November 11, 1879, describes the placement of a mirror on a stage to "render an actor or object gradually visible or invisible, at will," which, during a performance, would look to the audiences like a ghost or other phantom were interacting with the live actors. The chemist John Henry Pepper had originally patented it in England in 1863, which was in fact an improvement on another device called the Dircksian Phantasmagoria, invented by Henry Dircks, but which proved too unwieldly to be made to work on a typical stage, requiring a theater to be built specifically to accommodate it. The illusion worked by placing someone in a costume—often a simple white sheet—concealed from the view of the audience, sometimes in a hidden area of the orchestra pit. A piece of glass is angled at 45 degrees over the actor, which is also facing the audience. Light is shined onto the "ghost," which is then reflected toward the glass, creating the illusion that a spectral figure is onstage with the other characters. This can also be accomplished by placing the costumed figure off to the side of the stage and placing the angled glass onstage between the audience and the stage.

On Christmas Eve of 1862, the illusion debuted at London's Royal Polytechnic in the play "The Haunted House" by Charles Dickens. The show was immensely popular, claiming 250,000 visitors over five months. Posters for the event exclaimed: "The Ghost! The Ghost! The Ghost! See and Believe." Jim Steinmeyer, in his book *Hiding the Elephant*, recounts how Spiritualists would write to Pepper after his shows, applauding him for demonstrating the reality of the spirit world, a claim he never felt the need to correct.

Unlike Roberts and Pepper, however, Schröpfer wanted to create a sense of the supernatural in a ritual space, a kind of initiatory experience like what a shaman might fashion. The magic lantern and related devices easily produced altered states, especially for a public that had not yet seen motion pictures. The magic lantern's unique ability to function both as a stage magic prop and an opening into our occult imagination made it particularly useful in other ritual spaces. The lantern as a ritual device would eventually find its way into use by Freemasons, the experts of ceremony and initiation, during what is known as the Scottish rite. Even today, once Masons complete the first three degrees in their lodge (Entered Apprentice, Fellowcraft, and Master Mason), they can apply to be initiated into another complex series of degrees, from four to thirty-three. While the rituals have somewhat changed over time, one version of the Scottish rite, governed by what is called the Southern District, incorporates Pepper's Ghost so that during one performative moment of the rite, the apparition of a skeleton appears. The effect was also used as a way of teaching new candidates secret words by having them appear seemingly superimposed in the air. The simpler magic lantern was also incorporated, with scenes appearing and dissolving, and in one instance a man would turn into a skeleton to teach a symbolic lesson about mortality. The use of the magic lantern dates to at least 1892, where it is listed for sale in the *Catalogue for the Ancient and Accepted Scottish Rite*. The Masonic historian Wendy Rae Waszut-Barrett, in her remarkably erudite study on the Scottish rite ceremonial stagecraft, "Scenic Shifts upon the Scottish Rite Stage," makes note of the power of suggestion this kind of technology offers: "The illumination of secret words and phrases greatly improved as the message was magically revealed to the candidates."

The Victorian mind was particularly susceptible to being open to supernatural and occult realities, in part as a ballast against an increasing industrial and scientific worldview that had a disenchanting effect on people. What is known as the Occult Revival of the late nineteenth century would see the creation of several influential occult organizations, most important the Theosophical Society, founded by Helena Blavatsky (who believed Spiritualist mediums were wasting their talents by not asking spirits to expose their divine secrets) and the Hermetic Order of the Golden Dawn, which took the rites of Freemasonry and laced them with astrology, kabbalah, and ceremonial magic. More important, despite the hope by some that reason and science would usher in a new age, people did not want to give up their desire to be beguiled, and sometimes even frightened. Concurrently, the wilds of nature were slowly being contained and cordoned off by vast agricultural colonies in far-off places and zoos of nonnative creatures, and curiosity cabinets—the first museums—were established as places to safely gaze on the exotic, the prehistoric, and the dead. The great irony here is that as technology honed an increasingly mechanical perspective on the world, restraining our irrational or illogical side, it simultaneously offered new and novel ways with which to bewitch ourselves. While industry made the world smaller and closer, it was also understood to be larger than previously imagined.

The theater of the supernatural, whether in Schröpfer's private room, the medium's parlor, or Roberts's underground tomb, has been transformed by the next century's mediums of film and television, but their purpose and ability to beguile is the same. The 2007 film *Paranormal Activity* is a modern version of the spectral theater in which we, the audience, know that this is a fictional film layered with the meta idea that the movie is a "documentary" of a supernatural encounter. While not a great movie by critical discernment, it does elicit a creeping dread, sometimes merely using jump scares to provoke a response. Often what scares is the dissociation of what we are actually seeing. Characters Kate and her boyfriend, Micah, try to document ghostly phenomena in their home by setting up a video camera in their bedroom at night while they sleep. Over the course of many nights, the incidents become more and more dramatic (quiet clanking one night becomes thunderous clangs the next, a blanket being thrown over Kate seems almost playful until the evening when she is violently pulled from her bed and dragged down the hall by an invisible force). The subtext is that the activity is made worse by the very act of them trying to record it until finally Kate becomes possessed and kills Micah, all of which is captured on tape with a final "gotcha!" reveal. There is a kind of magic at work here where our perceptional limits are tested and we begin to "believe" what we are seeing is real. The effect may or may not linger once out on the street at the end of the movie, but the film's ability to create this rupture in our consciousness is something that can only be understood by the way in which technology offers us a new way to believe in the supernatural. The progenitor to these "found footage" movies, the 1999 film *Blair Witch Project*, uses the same ruse and effects to cajole the audience into participating as both audience and bearing witness to the ordeal of the actors.

In a 2013 performance during the Boing Boing event Ingenuity, the stage magician Ferdinando Buscema used the ancient technology of the Llullian wheel to demonstrate how the Renaissance technique, known as *ars combinatoria*, functions as a device for hacking our psychology. Ingenuity is an invitation-only gathering of hackers who demonstrate novel and creative uses of current tools to new ends. It brings engineering and performance together with entrepreneurial intentions. Ferdinando was an inspired choice of presenter. Born in 1975 in Crotone, Italy, Ferdinando trained as a mechanical engineer and, armed with a background in humanistic psychology and Hermetic traditions, works a full-time job as a magician designing what he bills as "magical experiences," and he sees a connection—a "resonance," he calls it—between these two seemingly separate careers. They align in his underlying interest of how things work and how to make things happen once you know the underlying technology. As an engineer interested in Hermetic traditions, Buscema is as comfortable with digital technology manuals as well as grimoires of esoterica. As he sees it, they are just different paths all flowing along the same spectrum of our desire to capture that part of the human experience that is beyond the phenomenal. Ferdinando's magic is intended to trigger a psychological and aesthetic mechanism, whose outcome is a sense of enchantment. In this regard, Ferdinando is achieving a similar purpose as that of the ART staging of *The Tempest* that used the technology of stage magic to represent occult magic, but expresses even more acutely what Shakespeare himself was attempting to do. Echoed in his stage direction for a "quaint device," Shakespeare is making explicit note that the magic performed both onstage and off is natural magic, not sorcery, which was believed during his time to be against the divine order. To achieve this, Ferdinando layers occult lore onto his presentations in hopes that even if an audience member is not consciously responsive to those themes, a seed is planted that may indeed still sprout.

The Llullian wheel Ferdinando used was designed and constructed by the artist and writer David Metcalfe. The device is a round wooden base with three layered discs hinged in the center. Ferdinando added LEDs around the circumference and installed a microprocessor. "My goal is to inhabit a space between this ancient occult and Hermetic tool and present-time technology." The wheel is connected to an application in his smartphone, which, he told me, "allows me to take someone's thoughts and read [them] through the app." During the act, Ferdinando asks an audience member to think up a short pass code and keep it in their mind. The wheel, Ferdinando tells the audience, can be used to crack any pass code, even one someone "is merely thinking about." The participant then stares into the device, keeping their password in their mind. Ferdinando then looks at his phone and then writes on a piece of cardboard, showing it to the startled audience member, who admits it was exactly the one he was thinking of. The trick is likely the same (secret) technique used by magicians throughout the ages, including someone like Samri Baldwin and other Spiritualist-esque performers. But Ferdinando's version is extraordinary because of the way he merges ancient and modern technology. He creates the suggestion that an occult device can read minds and then can somehow transmit that information onto Ferdinando's phone. It's almost as if we are more inclined to believe in supernatural powers when mediated through the use of technology. We accept, by default, that our electronic and digital devices work. Ferdinando is asking us to accept that they do something more than intended. And for one astonishing moment we do.

The Llullian wheel was the invention of Ramon Lull, a thirteenth-century Christian mystic and mathematician (during a time when these two disciplines were not mutually exclusive). The original device was a series of concentric circles, each containing a series of theological concepts. By turning each wheel, the corresponding elements would form new concepts that opened avenues of contemplation, supposedly revealing the total knowledge of creation. This technique was adopted by the Renaissance philosopher-mage and unabashed heretic Giordano

Bruno, who used them to create a vast magical cosmology. Using Lull's wheel, Bruno combined the Jewish kabbalistic concepts of the *sefirot*—the ten measurable divine properties that emanate from the unmeasurable Godhead—with the names of archangels and what were believed to be the levels of heaven, widening his cosmological understanding of the universe. Using a technique known as the Art of Memory, Bruno could then furnish the rooms of a mental palace with these corresponding concepts. This knowledge was, for Bruno, a method for accumulating divine wisdom to such a degree that he could invoke godly powers, including communicating with demons and divining the future. As Porta demonstrated, techniques and technologies of natural magic were a way of enchanting the mundane, of having people experience nature in a new way, and of having nature reveal something real but invisible. Bruno's magic was not simply a reflection of natural forces, nor was it like the Christian mages before him, who governed in part by a belief that their magic was a means to "prove the divinity of Christ," the scholar Frances Yates explains. Further, Bruno's magic was to become *equal* to God, which, by using the Llullian wheel along with the Art of Memory, could know "the multiplicity of appearances through having conformed his imagination to the archetypal images, and also has powers through this insight." Bruno believed these powers, as scholar Liberty Stanavage makes clear, could be demonstrated through performance, where the orator's skills can magically alter the audience's consciousness.

Ferdinando's use of these oratory memory skills was on display at another performance, this one in 2017 at the Magic Castle in Los Angeles, California. Here, Ferdinando described magic as an opportunity to "catch a glimpse of the cosmic order of the sphere, imposing order on the ocean of chaos upon which we are suspended." While

Ferdinando is not claiming his magic is occult in nature, he positions magic less like Porta, and more like the potent magic of Bruno. In one of Bruno's definitions of magic he writes that magic can produce "circumstances such that the actions of nature or of a higher intelligence occur in such a way as to excite wonderment by their appearances."

One of the tricks Ferdinando performed at the Magic Castle used an unbound copy of the occult text known as the Kybalion, which he believes contains "archetypical principles about how your mind works and how the universe works." The trick involves passing out various pages of the book, a "manual to access the higher mysteries," to the audience. One audience member is chosen to read to themselves the first line from the set of pages they were handed and choose a word that has significance for them. Through a series of questions about the sentence, Ferdinando can tell the person exactly what word they chose. Ferdinando personifies the principles of the Kybalion to create real occult resonances with and among the audience, to activate what he calls the "archetypal magician within."

The Kybalion situates itself here in some curious ways. The text, first published in 1908 and written by the pseudonymous "Three Initiates," purports to be writings of the Egyptian priest Hermes Trismegistus. The book presents "seven hermetic principles," describing the human mind as an agent in the spiritual laws of the universe, capable of effecting change in the world. One of the authors, along with occultist and New Thought pioneer William Walker Atkinson, is thought to possibly be the stage magician and Spiritualist Claude Alexander Conlin. Conlin, or C. Alexander, as he often presented himself, was well known for his performances, which included demonstrations of psychic powers, séances, and crystal gazing. Conlin's act is another location where this strange synergy between Spiritualism and stage magic took place, and where the difference in their techniques became blurry.

In 1921, Conlin published *The Life and Mysteries of the Celebrated Dr. Q*, in which he describes in detail how many Spiritualist and occult-infused stage demonstrations were performed by mediums and other magicians claiming to have arcane powers. In one anecdote, he recounts the police charging him with being a *fakir*, typically meaning a wandering holy man, but colloquially used to refer to someone pretending to have magical powers to dupe people out of their money. Conlin invited the police to come to his apartment so he could prove his occult powers. Conlin sat the chief of police and his officers in a circle, men to his left and right holding his wrists and pressing his feet down with theirs. With the lights off, a spirit emerged from the darkness with one-half of its face a skull, the other a woman. In fear and awe, the chief remarked, "We are a lot of damn fools; this man is genuinely possessed of the supernatural, and I fear we will all be cursed for trying to intimidate him." But Conlin explains the trick: he hid a specially built hose in his pocket when the light went out that could inflate a balloon decorated with luminous paint. Nevertheless, the purpose of his book, Conlin writes, is not to discount all supernatural phenomena, but to "separate the wheat from the chaff." Conlin makes it clear he accepts certain testimonies that the dead can communicate with the living, but that he wants to expose the *fakirs* so "that it may help in the research of genuine psychic phenomena."

Ferdinando invokes and then elevates the person of a magician like Conlin (and the magus Bruno), who debunked Spiritualism while still playing coy about the source of their powers by layering his performance with occult references as a way of reminding people about these aspects of our imaginations. He achieves this by making a literal demonstration of the concepts he presents. Just as the origins of theater and performance lie in that moment when the concept of Dionysus becomes literalized in the performance and the audience is initiated, Ferdinando sees his own craft as a form of ritual. He admits it doesn't work all the time. Some audience members would say, Ferdinando recalled, "Well, he did a nice job. The guy is nice and smart and knowledgeable." Others will be more taken by the show and say, "Wow, that was beautiful." And then there will be the ones who allow themselves to be transformed, to be enchanted.

Buscema contends that the dimensions of the so-called "trick" and "effect" belong to two distinct domains. The "trick" is the medium, or the tool, the *technology* behind the curtain that is required for the magic to transpire. The "effect" is the outcome, whose goal is amazement and surprise. He does not hope that the audience will suspend their disbelief; he intends for the magic to *raze* disbelief. According to Buscema, "No matter how advanced our technological artifacts will be, the need for magic and mystery—being something primal and archetypical—will always be part of the human experience."

This sentiment is shared by Joshua Madara, a self-described "technomancer" who is a practicing occultist but draws directly from the traditions of stage magic to design and build magical technologies. But unlike stage magicians, whose operative mechanisms are jealously guarded secrets, Joshua wants to expose everything through using open-source technologies because, as Joshua explained to me over video chat: "I don't think the technology is where the magic is. I think the magic is in what we make, what we perform, and what we do with it."

Just as Ferdinando was trained as an engineer, Joshua's background is in computers and his magical practice is intimately tied to that vocation. After high school, Joshua did vocational training in industrial electronics and robotics. In 1995, he joined the Builders of the Adytum, a religious organization founded by occultist Paul Foster Case in 1922 that teaches the "Tradition of the Western Mysteries" and offers correspondence courses on tarot, kabbalah, and other esoteric subjects. Joshua's interest in esoterica waned for a bit as he began to focus on a career in computers. Around 2002, he learned about an online class being taught through the author of the infamous Illuminatus! Trilogy and counterculture hero Robert Anton Wilson's Maybe Logic Academy, an online community of occultists. It was here Joshua was introduced to an occult practice known as chaos magic (often rendered as "magick").

Chaos magic has its origins in the life and work of Austin Osman Spare, a magician and artist who developed a technique called sigil magic. Even within occult circles, Spare was a bit of a rebel, eschewing magical societies and fraternities in favor of a focus on the individual's own revelatory potential. Sigil magic is a method whereby a person writes down some intention on a piece of paper (find a job, meet a lover, win the Nobel Prize) and begins to reduce the sentence or phrase letter by letter, first removing vowels, for example, then letters having more than one occurrence, and then layering the remaining letters on top of one another, working them into an artistic form or shape that suggests the intent to the psyche. The sigil is then meditated on, and often burned so that only a mental image of the symbol remains, the original sentence extinguished, except as it exists in the unconscious. Spare's ideas were later amplified by British occultist Peter Carroll, who religion scholar Colin Duggan explains sought to align magic with science by emphasizing experimentation. Carroll wanted to do away with what he saw as a dogma infecting contemporary occult practice, where once magic had, as Carroll writes, "a strong antinomian flavor." What distinguishes chaos magic from other types of occult practice is that belief is simply a tool one uses to achieve outcomes. Chaos practitioners worship whichever gods or spirits they choose as a way of creating mental maps for the goals they have in front of them, at the same time rejecting any idea of objective or universal truth. The technique, Carroll writes, is one of "visualization, the creation of thought entities and altered states of consciousness" that bring about the desired results.

Always on the lookout for the intersection of technology and magic, Joshua began to investigate cybernetics—systems that create changes in their environment and then respond to those changes—and came to realize he needed to begin actually making these kinds of technomagical objects he had been imagining. "There is some kind of a Luciferian ideal to the hacker and the maker thing," he told me. This is not the Lucifer that is attached to the Christian mythology of the devil or Satan, but Lucifer the "light bearer," often referred to in esoteric thought as a symbol of enlightenment. For the mystic philosopher and architect Rudolf Steiner, Lucifer is a metaphor for the human faculty, "when something in the world demands an answer and we are thrown back entirely upon our own resources." As a maker and occultist, the key for Joshua is experimentation, something he found possible with both maker technologies and chaos magic.

The maker movement can be traced to various subcultures of the 1960s and '70s, particularly by way of the *Whole Earth Catalog*, the back-to-land movement, and punk fanzine ethos. They were attempts to rebel against the idea that invention and innovation were privy to corporations or the academy. From these rose the Silicon Valley hacker and cyberpunk culture of the nineties. Gareth Branwyn, writer and editor, and a pioneer of both online culture and the maker movement, told me by e-mail that many of the founders of maker culture and the founding editors of *Make:* magazine—the essential quarterly text of DIY enthusiasts—hailed from these subcultures, out of which a like-minded people congregated. Dale Dougherty, founder of *Make:* magazine and Maker Faire, Gareth explained, gave a label—"maker"—to people who want to learn about how the technology in their lives works, and "who like to tinker, to fix things rather than throw them away." Gareth quoted the hacker ethic, which extends to the hacker or maker who must "yield to the hands-on imperative." Then Gareth described the corresponding tension between magic and the supernatural interfaced with conventional religion institutions: "The established inventor-world in some ways feels threatened by the maker movement because it embraces an open source ethos." Exploring the possibility of supernatural realties with technology also requires an open-source ethos, as it requires reimaging the accepted way certain devices are supposed to function.

In the early days of the Internet, users of an online chat protocol called Internet Relay Chat (IRC) discovered they often shared occult interests and formed virtual covens in which they would perform rituals, but they were still beholden to classical ideas about both technology and magic. Joshua explained that this model—what he calls the classic interface of screen, keyboard, and mouse—is still dominant today. This standard was found even in fantastical accounts of technology and religion. In Arthur C. Clarke's 1953 story "The Nine Billion Names of God," a group of computer scientists build and program a computer for a group of Tibetan monks whose purpose is to count all the names of God, something the monks would not be able to do in their lifetime. After months of the computer processing the names, one night the scientists see the light of the stars disappearing one by one. This story perfectly encapsulates one of Clarke's most famous and often quoted dicta: "Any sufficiently advanced technology is indistinguishable from magic." The story of the monks also prefigures one of the key ways we would come to imagine how computers would be inserted into a supernatural context. The film director John Carpenter's 1987 gnostic horror film *Prince of Darkness* imagines a group of scientists using a computer to reveal the true nature of Satan and the greater evil known as the Anti-God. Here, the computer is simply doing complex calculations of strange data, but is not in any way an occult device.

Wanting to go further than just having a machine do the magical work, Joshua taught himself computer processing, the kid-friendly programming language from MIT known as Scratch, and microcontrollers like Arduino. His intention is to ultimately create a multimedia tool kit for magicians. One of Joshua's most striking creations is the performance of ritual dramas with robots. "Half of what I'm attempting to do is to influence the audience," he told me during our conversation. "The other half is more mysterious." The magician—or in this case the robomancer—stands holding a wand while facing a small, mobile robot. The robomancer asks a question and intuitively moves the wand in a symbolic representation of her query. The robot responds by ambulating around the ritual space, and like reading tea leaves or entrails, she discerns some kind of answer to her query. In another ceremony, a robot acts out a fetish—a magical totem—used to contain the magician's "life force." The robomancer says a prayer and then presses the palm of her hand on a specially prepared metal panel that has been wired to the robot. Suddenly, the once-still robot powers on.

Joshua is loath to have people try to understand these rituals as I described here: "It is all too easy for ritual magic to appear as shitty

performance art. I prefer it be experienced by those participating in it."
During these performances, Joshua believes, the ritual space reflects
the internal and psychological changes that are happening within the
magician. The real magic is what takes place between the audience and
the space and the magician, and how it all comes together. Joshua worries that people are too quick to dismiss occult activity as merely psychological. "I want to preserve the mystery, the possibility that there's
something going on there that we have to learn about in a different way
than we're used to." This is what technology affords. It becomes a new
medium through which to imagine the unbelievable. In a ritual setting,
for example, these are states often achieved with music and drumming,
chanting, and prolonged gazing. "But, with technology and computa-
tional technology, you make responsive ritual spaces where the lights
change or the music changes or the mood changes depending on where
the participants are in the space." In a setting like this, the space can
feel as if it is magically alive and responsive. "Somebody's not stopping
the ritual to go press a button somewhere to make the music start,"
Joshua said.

Stage magic forms an important aspect of Joshua's own thinking.
Watching stage magic involves a series of complicated mental gymnas-
tics. The audience knows that what is happening onstage is an illusion,
such as sawing a person in half, but since we don't know how the trick
is done, we give over to our ancient instincts, which believe, even on an
unconscious level, that genuine magic is taking place. At the same
time, Joshua explained, we still maintain that alongside this there is no
real enchantment. This push and pull of reason and unreason are at the
heart of all our engagements with the supernatural, even when we
know they are staged. This is true even when we are watching a movie
about ghosts or other hauntings. In the case of Joshua's technomancy,

the situation is reversed. When he designs ritual elements involving computers or electronics, he knows, like the stage magician, exactly how they function and how to use them. "When the ritual is performed," he said, "I must forget that and allow myself to be enchanted." Yet the stage magician still haunts offstage when other people participate in the rituals. The people become spectators to Joshua's inventions and often will be asked how the effects were done. Of course, he tells them, "A magician never reveals his secrets."

Informed by the spirit rappers of Spiritualism, Joshua placed a microcontroller with a little knocker attached underneath a simple table. The device can respond to voice commands, and it contains an RFID reader so that it can detect, and then respond to, when different objects are placed on the table. But it also depends on randomness: Joshua is not entirely in control of how the device will respond during a séance.

Directly inspired by one of the most famous artifacts of divinatory technology, Joshua is also working on a talking skull. The talking skull is a classic stage magic trick whereby the magician displays a skull on a pedestal. The magician then asks the skull a series of questions, which it "answers" by clicking its jaw open and closed. The skull can also be made to turn to look in the direction of someone in the audience who volunteers to ask a question. The June 1923 issue of *Popular Mechanics* offers a firsthand report of a version of the skull—called "Balsamo"— who is asked by an audience member if the skull has seen her dead brother on the "other side." When the skull clicks in the affirmative, the woman cries out, "Tell him . . . Dad knows he was not a coward." The mechanical skull as divinatory device has its origins in an object— never proven to exist—known as the brazen head. The philosopher and scientist Francis Bacon has been the object of many strange theories, not the least of which is the speculation that he was the author of

Shakespeare's plays. During his lifetime, however, he was often accused of being a magician, partly because of his work in scientific investigations suggested, as Allison Kavey writes, "the search for control over the natural world." In the play *Friar Bacon and Friar Bungay*, written by Robert Greene around 1589 and first staged in England in 1592, the character of Francis Bacon is a powerful mage who creates a brazen head, controlled by the magic of the planets and able to divine the future. In the play, the head is ultimately destroyed, but the rumor of a real magic head firmly attached itself to various occult speculations regarding Bacon's life. Joshua intends to program his skull so that it can have different voices and speak various prophetic declarations and will be able to interact with the table through wireless radio.

In the case of the table and the skull, Joshua is able to exert a level of control within the randomization. But what if a computer is actually performing the magic? There are examples of automatic magics throughout history, well before computers, objects that are preloaded with spells or hexes that will activate at a certain time, such as a cursed tomb that activates when opened by an intruder or a heat-powered Tibetan prayer wheel that automatically turns by a candle flame. Joshua notes the most well known is the trope of the *Sorcerer's Apprentice*, where the magician—Mickey Mouse in the most famous version—commands a broom to sweep the house but soon can no longer control it. Related to all this, of course, is the question of the locus of magical agency: Does it come from within or without? Are occult forces real outside the imagination? As Joshua told me, many of the same questions come up regarding computers: Are their actions their own or their programmers'? "I come from a background of embedded computing and robotics," he told me. "For me, a computer is much more than a general-purpose PC. And now, with maker technology it's easy to do an occult thing that blows away what anybody was doing in the 1990s, and it's using a technology that a twelve-year-old kid can use." Practicing occultists might tell you, however, that there can be no supernormal function until you alter your consciousness. Joshua believes that technology can be a means to open a channel to the numinous, to realms beyond the merely physical.

———

The Tempest performance at the ART was woven with all the historical threads of natural magic, the late-nineteenth- and early-twentieth-century staging of mediums, the spirit shows from Schröpfer to Pepper, and the subsequent popularity of supernatural "found footage" in current movies. All this unlocked the notion for me that the experience of the supernatural does not depend on its truthfulness. We possess the ability to enter the occult parlors of our imaginations, to transcend our rational states of mind and return whole. Even when we can discern the mechanical device behind a phenomenon, its value is in no way lessened.

There is a quality inherent in the occult imagination that wants us to remain in a liminal space. Nate described this to me in terms of stage magic. "Magic demands that the audience comes in at full intelligence," he explained, because the magician understands the spectator knows the illusions aren't real. "And yet, it looks like it's real. I'm sharing the same physics with you in the room," Nate said. It's remarkable that we can exist in two states at the same time. Our minds are like thaumatropes, those little toys where a disc with a picture on both sides is flipped over by pulling on two strings attached to its sides. A thaumatrope with a bird on one side and a cage on the other will create the optical illusion that the bird is in the cage. Technology functions in the same way, being an extension of our rational selves and our capacity for invention and craftsmanship, but it also has long provided a way to extend ourselves into the irrational, toward the world of spirit and magic. Sometimes we are left feeling unsettled, even when the source of the mystery is known. As we saw, this has been called the uncanny valley, a psychological location where the real and the unreal coexist. And there is a kind of technology where the uncanny is made visible and has haunted people for generations: spirit photography, early motion picture techniques used to create ghostly images, and pop culture's fascination with glimpsing the supernatural and how visual-oriented technology became the locus for supernatural and otherworldly manifestations.

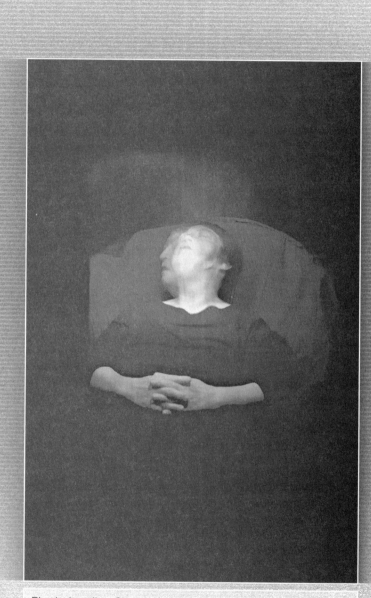

Physical medium Sharon Harvey in trance, as her spirit guide asks to be photographed; Enfield, England, 2013

CHAPTER 4

The Ghost and
Ms. Taggart

In an octagon-shaped house on the outskirts of Lily Dale in upstate New York, I sat with the photographer Shannon Taggart in a room whose windows had been shrouded with heavy black cloth. The door was similarly covered so that not even the slightest bit of light would peek through the cracks. Along with Shannon and me, there were twenty or so other people seated in folding metal chairs that encircled the room along the walls. In the front of the room stood a large curtained rectangular box, known as a spirit cabinet. Inside the cabinet was a single high-backed wooden chair, and on the floor around the chair were various small drums and horns. People spoke in quiet voices while we waited for the séance to begin.

I had seen the medium a few minutes before, outside smoking a cigarette. He seemed a bit shy, not quite standoffish but clearly did not want to make small talk before he performed. When he finally came into the room, he was self-possessed, with the demeanor of a man about to attempt a high-wire act. He gave us all very specific instructions, and warned that to veer from them in any way was extremely dangerous. Once the lights were off and the door closed, no one was to leave the room, nor could we, under any circumstances, get up from our seats. If we felt something come near us, we should not reach out to it. We had already placed our cell phones, keys, and watches in a basket outside the door; we should not attempt to sneak in an electronic device. A breach of these rules, even the smallest, could result in terrible consequences and could prove fatal to the medium. One young woman was starting to think she might not want to stay, and had to be reassured that as long as we did as we were instructed, everything would be okay.

The door was closed, its edges sealed with more of the heavy black cloth so no light could bleed through. The medium sat in the high-backed chair and two volunteers bound his wrists to the wooden arms with straps. A gag was placed over this mouth, the curtains of the cabinet were drawn shut and all the lights were extinguished. After a few tense, quiet minutes, there was the sound of a chair scraping and banging on the floor. It grew louder and louder until it was suddenly silent, followed by a boom like a sudden exhalation, and then the room was filled with sound. The beat of a drum encouraged a bit of rhythmic clapping, and the noise of feet stomping, until a pained, raspy roar took over. Long cardboard horns, known as spirit trumpets, which had been decorated with glow-in-the-dark tape, floated and soared around us. The sound of a slide whistle startled me. It was otherworldly, despite being slightly comical. The unexpectedness of it was also because it was clear that before the lights had gone out, a slide whistle was not one of the props that was laid out by the medium's feet. It was important that we had seen what the medium had access to, how he sat, and the way he was bound and gagged. Even the floating trumpets were not so strange as the enigmatic noise of the slide whistle.

We were then introduced to various spirits, including a child that added a bit of creepy unease, but the leader was a spirit with a deep, booming voice. As each spirit revealed itself, the room erupted in encouragement, with some of the participants eliciting a call akin to witnessing in a Christian revival meeting. For the dedicated Spiritualists in the room, the voices of the spirits were not startling but recognizable, like seeing an old friend after a long absence. There is joy, and a moment of surprise, but then you carry on as usual. People here were not expecting or hoping for transcendence or an unexpected encounter with the supernatural. Spiritualism accepts the reality of spirits interacting with the living as commonplace. They cheered, clapped along to the music, laughed at the terrible jokes that the spirits made. I was trying to find the ineffable, but the energy of the people around me rejected any feeling of the uncanny. I was ready and open to being altered, but it never came, not during the séance at least. The sense of enchantment, of having been in the presence of a rift in the space where spirits and mortals can interact, wouldn't come for me until the experience was filtered through technology, in this case a digital SLR.

Shannon had arranged to take photographs of the séance with the hopes to capture images of ectoplasm, a kind of spiritual goo that—although rarely seen—has been known to extrude from human orifices such as the mouth and nostrils. The medium couldn't guarantee the spirits would allow her to take pictures, but he suggested she have her camera and other equipment ready in case permission was granted. Even this, however, had to be done under strict controls. Before the séance began, the camera's battery had to be removed and everything else placed under her chair. Under no circumstances was Shannon to attempt to use the camera until she was given specific instructions on when and how it would be permissible.

After an hour of various sounds such as drumming and whistles, conversations with the spirits and the participants about love and faith, and continued commands to clap, sing, and then to sit quietly, the spirit in charge told Shannon it would be possible for her to take photographs. "Listen precisely to every word of instruction," the voice warned. "Is that clear?" Shannon agreed, and the spirit continued in a tone that flashed a degree of flirtatiousness, "In a moment you will be asked to attach your battery and then turn it on." When the order was given, Shannon did as she was told and then asked if she could set the camera on a tripod. All the while the participants were sitting quietly, so as not to disturb whatever machinations were happening in the space between the worlds to allow a camera to become an element in the séance. The spirit agreed to the tripod, and then said, "At no point are you to point your device anywhere near the cabinet." Shannon would be allowed to take "snapshots" only and then had to immediately "disengage the battery." Once everything was set up, the spirit told a helper sitting near the cabinet to light a small tea candle that sat on a dish near the front of the cabinet and then to start the CD player and to turn the volume up. Once the song ended, Shannon would then be allowed to turn on the camera. "Do not engage your batteries until the song has finished," the spirit said in its most serious manner thus far. Everyone sang along to "Sweet Caroline," as if we were at a Red Sox game and not in a room filled with the talkative spirits of the dead, while we waited, a slight tension in the room as we watched the faint flickering movement of Shannon while she prepared her tripod and camera.

It appeared, at least on this night in the darkened room of the octagonal house, that the ghostly denizens were not so predisposed to having their pictures taken as they'd once been. The dramatic decision whether Shannon would be allowed to take photographs, and then the detailed directions that followed, suggested that the spirit world was mistrustful of the camera. This suspicion of technology and what it might reveal was not what I expected. While this kind of physical mediumship—the production of ectoplasm, floating instruments—is certainly rarer than it was in the nineteenth and early twentieth centuries, the contemporary interest in ghosts, haunted houses, and other supernatural phenomena has been made increasingly popular by television shows like *Ghost Hunters* and films such as *The Conjuring*. I expected that those in the spirit business would invite the camera as a source of potential documentary evidence, if not an excellent marketing tool. Moreover, there was a time when mediums, and the souls that they channeled, were dependent on the photographer's craft. In the nineteenth century, the two were inexorably linked, and in some cases the photograph itself was the true medium, a tool used by the spirits to become manifest. Using special lenses for seeing spirits and related otherworldly denizens was a decidedly nineteenth- and early-twentieth-century development. In Arthur Conan Doyle's slim 1922 volume *The Coming of the Fairies*, the creator of the beloved character Sherlock Holmes speculates that we might one day invent a pair of "psychic spectacles" that would allow us to see beings whose existence is invisible due to their vibrating at different frequencies. Like many Spiritualists of his time, Doyle believed that the world was populated by spirits, fairies, and other supernatural entities. Only a select sensitive few— mediums—had the faculties to apprehend them, but human ingenuity could allow everyone access to the occult secrets of the cosmos. And Doyle had proof. The shutter speed of a camera, for example, was able to capture the playful interaction of fairies and young girls in the idyllic woods of Cottingley, England. Doyle's belief that a camera could see what the unaided eye could not represent an important moment in the relationship between technology and spiritual ideas. Doyle's willingness to embrace technology—even as science undermined the substance of his spiritual beliefs—marks an essential quality of the supernatural imagination. When Doyle was presented with evidence that the fairy photographs were faked, he still insisted that with the right technology, human beings would have access to another level of reality. We had conquered the land with the steam engine and could communicate across vast distances through the air using wireless transmitters. It would not require much more inventiveness to sweep open the veil that separates our world from the hidden realm of the spirit. Doyle's imagined spectacles are a mediator, a means through which mortals could withstand seeing the divine realm. Doyle's glasses are also objects of power, to be crafted by human beings in order to wrest secrets from nature and to place mankind at the zenith.

Those who accepted that photography could capture images of the presence of spirits often pointed to X-rays as an example of where the unseen could be rendered visible. More important, it was believed that the spirits themselves "directed" the medium to be photographed. In 1911, a decade before Doyle's public declaration, James Coates published *Photographing the Invisible*, in which he refers to the "Intelligences in the Invisible," writing, "Intelligent messages can only come from intellects capable of sending them." Thus, the spirits are participating in the capturing of their forms, and the attempt would be impossible without "cooperation."

Spiritualism arose at a time when photography—and other technological advances such as the telegraph—would elevate it beyond becoming merely another form of wishful religious fancy. Spiritualism was not only moral, it was rational. And unlike other beliefs in the supernatural, it could be documented. It could be *proved*. Up until the time of Spiritualism and the first spirit photographs, there was little in American religious practice that would suggest that people of faith would one day accept that technology could capture the reality of the divine and the supernatural. It wouldn't be until the mid-twentieth century when Biblical literalists would try to merge scientific concepts with Biblical history in order to "prove" concepts such as the Flood as well as provide ways to reconcile how dinosaurs and records of early humans square with accounts found in Genesis. Nevertheless, there is a quality inherent in Protestantism—the denomination out of which Spiritualism arose—that recognizes the value of human labor as a measure of salvation. The spiritual irony of Protestantism—and in particular Calvinism—as described by the early-twentieth-century sociologist Max Weber, is that no amount of religious practice can affect whether one has received God's grace. Therefore, the Christian man or woman must *believe* they have been chosen by God to receive salvation, and yet "intense worldly activity is recommended as the most suitable means" to feel confident that they are among the chosen. Spiritualism absorbed this tension masterfully, at once believing that any medium with sufficient skill to be able to communicate and materialize the souls of the dead was chosen to be a divine instrument without effort on their part, and second that the work of the medium was proof of their God-given gift. Many Christians still saw Spiritualism as the work of the devil, a form of magic explicitly forbidden in the Bible ("Do not turn to mediums or wizards; do not seek them out, to be defiled by them," Leviticus 19:31). It was not the spirits of the dead that are manifesting they believed, but devils and fallen angels whose purpose is "toward working mischief against the well-disposed, and the debauchery of those over whom they gain absolute control."

Spiritualism and its supporters fought back. In his 1896 book *The Religion of Modern Spiritualism and Its Phenomena*, Dr. William Cleveland asserted mediums are controlled by God's angels, not the rebellious type who followed the devil in his retreat from heaven. More important, he writes, "Jesus was a medium and devoted Spiritualist. He proclaimed it everywhere and on all occasions, and for his daring was nailed to the cross." While this God-given gift would wait centuries before it would reveal itself again, the proof Cleveland believed was demonstrated in Hydesville, New York's Fox sisters, whose special talents would announce that "death has gained a new victory; hell had lost its sting."

The emphasis on observable phenomena that characterized Spiritualism reinforced what religious historian Ann Braude describes as the movement's "claim to be scientific." Braude explains that some mediums and their followers saw themselves as scientists of the spirit world, merely an aspect of "the nature of reality." This relationship between the spirit and the medium was often described in technological terms, an important way to align Spiritualism with the very science that was undermining religion's hold. The technology of optics, having recently opened a once-invisible world with the microscope and X-ray, offered a range of metaphors with which to describe mediumship. Allan Kardec, known as the "human telescope" and author and father of Spiritism (a belief in reincarnation as a means for spiritual evolution), wrote that "mediumship has been for the spirit world what the telescope has been for the heavenly world and the microscope for the infinitely small world." Technology is a means through which we conquer our own material limitations. Just as mediumship offers the selfsame mastery of the spiritual, "the microscope and the telescope are equally striking protests against the limitations of sight," the medium and Spiritualist Horace Leaf writes in his 1926 *The Psychology and Development of Mediumship*. Spiritualism collapses the distance between the living and the dead.

The emotional aspect of Spiritualism, coupled with an explosion of technological innovation, would extend the metaphor of the medium as a lens into literal acceptance that a camera could in fact capture the spirit world. Just as the microscope and the telescope exposed the hidden aspects of the material world, it was not so implausible that the wondrous extraordinary technology of the camera might reveal another hidden realm. Grief or loss induced people to not only seek out mediums who might channel the voices of their deceased loved ones, but to find those who could capture their forms in the new and wondrous technology of the camera.

The implication that the spirits require the mechanism of the camera to become visible might suggest that their power is limited, but for those who believed, it made sense that the veil between worlds was not easily lifted without an extension of the human operator, a tool. At the same time, there was a tension between wanting to accept with some confidence the science of how photography works and the "truth" of the spirit images. To this end, it was often put forth that not only did the spirit wish to be photographed, but that some other supernatural activity exploited the camera's own limitations. James Coates writes in his later 1922 work *Seeing the Invisible*:

> Whether this transference is from the spirit side or from our side, one thing is certain, that these photographs resembling the likeness of departed friends are obtained—nay, more, are deposited

on the photographic plates—independently of the photographic procedure necessary to obtain the likeness of the visible sitter.

Attempts were made to use contemporary scientific principles to at least suggest that even supernatural entities were subject to the laws of physics, even if those laws were not yet discovered or understood. In the July 1897 issue of the Spiritualist journal *Borderland,* an account given of a spirit who attempted a thorough explanation is worth quoting at length:

> When such results are obtained they are due to the excitation of certain invisible rays or forces which would give the appearance or effect of light, very much in the same way as what are known as "X" rays. We say, *when* such results are obtained, for they are entirely dependent on certain knowledge possessed by spirits as to the chemical constitution of matter and the method of producing the particular vibrations requisite to effect the desired results. It is practically impossible for us to explain the process to you, because you would have to stand on our side of life and watch the operation in order to understand any description we might give you.

The phrase "on our side of life" encapsulates the belief that the denizens of the otherworld whose images are captured on film are not dead but have simply passed on to another realm, a place where forces can cross over and provoke our technology to behave in new and curious ways.

It was in 1862, however, that the November 1 issue of the *Banner of Light* had received proof of the promise of their "spirit friends that in due time the mundane world would be startled" by what the writer calls a "new phase of Spiritual Manifestation." This "spirit power" was in the form of a photograph, first reported by their sister publication, the *Herald of Progress*. The photograph was taken by William Mumler, an engraver in Boston who had been experimenting with a camera at a local studio when he discovered one of the negatives revealed a ghostly figure. One of the studio's photographers explained that the glass plate used in taking the picture must have been dirty, and so an afterimage had appeared on the new negative. Mumler was satisfied until he was visited by a Spiritualist friend who became so taken by the photograph, he asked Mumler to write on the back the circumstances by which the photograph had been taken and to sign his name. Mumler was happy to oblige, thinking he was playing a bit of a joke on his friend. In his autobiography, Mumler writes that he "never dreamed of any publicity being given to it."

The *Banner of Light*, believing that Mumler's photograph was the "incontrovertible evidence of the truth that spiritual communications are what they claim to be, viz: actual manifestations of the 'dead' to the 'living,'" called Mumler a "medium and artist," and to the surprise of Mumler, published the address of the photography studio where he first took the picture, Mrs. H. F. Stuart's Photographic Gallery on 258 Washington Street. Soon after, Mumler describes being inundated with requests to produce spirit photographs, but it was an encounter with an unnamed "scientist from Cambridge" who told Mumler that the original explanation for how the spirit image appeared on the negative could not have been an aftereffect of the glass plate, as was previously described by his colleague. Convinced, or so it would seem, Mumler would go on to produce hundreds of spirit photographs, including a portrait of Mary Todd Lincoln that shows the ghostly figure of the sixteenth president of the United States, seven years after his assassination. (It's worth noting that this incident was particularly troublesome for Mrs. Lincoln. The photograph not only increased her already abiding beliefs in Spiritualism but, at least according to public perception, pushed her over the edge. She had what she thought were prophetic dreams, heard voices, and eventually was institutionalized for a brief time.)

As was the case with any demonstration of mediumship, skeptical scientists and other professionals sought to discredit any suggestions of evidence of spirit contact, but in the case of Mumler it was one of his own patrons, the Boston Spiritualist H. F. Gardner, who began to suspect a deception was at play. In a letter to the *Banner of Light*, Gardner expressed sadness at discovering that ghostly images seen in some of Mumler's photographs were people still living, and that despite his resolute belief that spirits can indeed be photographed, Mumler's ability should be met with skepticism. This would begin the souring of Mumler's reputation in Boston, and he soon moved to New York City in the hopes of starting anew. For about a year, between 1868 and 1869, Mumler carried on, garnering quite a lot of local press, until a fraud investigation was opened by the city. Mumler found himself in court for what historian Louis Kaplan describes as a "machine" of "urban tabloid journalism and the commercial desire to crank out sensational stories and to sell newspapers," with the result being a complete shift in the public perception of spirit photography. Mumler was acquitted but even the judge admitted he believed Mumler a fraud despite the lack of evidence. But the final blow was when the Photographic Section of the American Institute wrote a letter to the *Philadelphia Photographer* asserting that spirit photography is a "matter of trickery" and to "condemn all such methods" as being an attempt to dupe the public. Mumler never wavered in his own defense, and continued to say that he was merely a vessel through which the spirit world made itself known.

Mumler's photographs don't stand up well today, but despite what appears to be some sort of superimposition method, the images are alluring. Most follow a typical schema. A person sits for a portrait on a high-backed chair and above and behind them a milky white, ghostly human form hovers, often with one arm resting on the subject. In each photo, the subject is completely unaware of any supernatural occurrence, suggesting that without the photo there would be no indication of any phenomena having taken place. No one appears startled or even nervous. Only when the image is developed is the instrument of mediumship activated.

Spirit photography did not end with the trial, though it certainly did not garner the same public sympathy and attention as it had when Mumler was working at full tilt. There are several reasons this relationship changed. The first is that it became harder to produce spirit photographs that were not easily debunked. As photographic technology advanced, so did our understanding of the ways film and prints could be manipulated in the lab, and even in the camera itself. As early as the 1870s, Spiritualists were finding themselves torn between what they fervently hoped was evidence of their experiences and beliefs and the almost amateurish way that spirit photos could be faked. Frederick Hudson was the first documented spirit photographer in England, but quickly found himself at the center of this debate. His images show shrouded figures interacting with the sitter, looking down on them or sometimes causing other phenomena, such as causing a table to lift. Quickly into his career, Hudson was being accused of fraud, with many photographers easily demonstrating how Frederick could have had pre-prepared photographic plates of someone in costume that were then superimposed onto the new picture. For those Spiritualists who either refused to accept they could be so easily deceived or those whose faith in the process was so ardent, other explanations were offered, such as the spirit imprinted its form on the plate before the photo was taken. Spirit photography became increasingly boutique until the adherents of Spiritualism no longer believed it offered any value for their religious practice, or in some cases had any real worth at all.

The British naturalist Alfred Russel Wallace, known today as the once-uncredited figure behind helping shape Charles Darwin's evolutionary theory, was also an ardent Spiritualist who had been photographed by Hudson showing a figure Wallace believed was his deceased mother. In 1891, Wallace wrote to the Society of Psychical Research (SPR) asking them to take spirit photography seriously, which he believed was "perhaps, the most unassailable demonstration it is possible to obtain of the objective reality of spiritual forms." The SPR, founded in 1882, attempted to use controlled scientific methods and reasoning to investigate what might be authentic spiritual and paranormal phenomena. One of the SPR's most prominent members was Eleanor Mildred Sidgwick, who took up Wallace's challenge by writing a lengthy response in the *Proceedings of the SPR*. Looking at almost every documented case of spirit photography up to that time, Sidgwick could show how each one could have been fabricated. "It appeared to me that, after eliminating what might certainly or probably be attributed to trickery," she wrote, "the remaining evidence was hardly sufficient in amount to establish even a *prima facie* case for investigation," effectively closing the door on the SPR even taking up spirit photography as worthy of inquiry.

The ability to fake spirit photographs was playfully demonstrated in a wonderfully self-referential film from 1898, *Photographing a Ghost* by George Albert Smith. In the film, a photographer tries to photograph a ghost, only to have it appear and disappear at will. This and other special effects used by people like George Méliès demonstrated that with enough technical proficiency, the most fantastical images could be produced on film. In his 1898 film *The Four Troublesome Heads*, Méliès removes his head and places it on a table, where it turns and speaks. Méliès himself then goes under the table to show that there is no one hiding underneath, as if the appearance of two heads is not the amazing feat. Historian of stage magic Jim Steinmeyer explains the simple technique used here of double exposing a strip of film. It was then a matter of "aligning the image so that the head appeared to rest on the tabletop." Because of these kinds of popular entertainments, belief in spirit photographs was sure to wane, and as more startling effects were seen on film, people turned away from séances and visits to Spiritualist parlors. The modern world was intruding on the spiritual, and while technology was being shown as having divine purpose, its other uses were beginning to blur the reality of the spirit photograph.

For myself I felt more of a sense of wonder watching the Méliès film than the live séance I attended with Shannon, which offered almost no sense of the amazement. Yet this isn't to suggest that some of the famous spirit photographs of the late nineteenth and early twentieth centuries don't offer moments of wonder and raise questions as to what was occurring. Often, however, the use of technology reveals a limitation rather than a deepening of the Spiritualist phenomenon. It's the difference between watching a sleight of hand magician on the street two feet in front of you, and watching a magic act on television where it's impossible to suspend disbelief and enter the almost trancelike state that occurs when you see a live magic show. The irony that I was to experience at Lily Dale was that Shannon's photographs were what astonished me and opened the possibility that indeed an unveiling between worlds had occurred.

―――――――――

Standing outside of the Lily Dale Museum, Shannon pointed to the doorway of the building and told me this was where she took a photo of a woman named Dorothy. The image was taken without special filters, with a normal exposure. The photo, called "Dorothy with Bob's Orb," shows Dorothy with a bluish sphere hovering over her right shoulder. Shannon explained that at the time she saw nothing unusual when she was taking Dorothy's picture. It wasn't until she was developing the film that she saw the orb. Shannon showed the photo to Dorothy, who remarked, "Oh, that's Bob," her then-deceased husband. "I thought I'd spend one summer doing a very journalistic project, a straightforward piece about this town that's so unique," Shannon told me. The photo of Bob's spirit changed her motivation. "Lily Dale ended up presenting a lot of mystery to me, and the more I dug the more I found."

Before the séance, Shannon gave me a tour of the village of Lily Dale. The summer season had not yet started up, the time of the year when believers and skeptics alike descend upon Lily Dale looking for a supernatural assignation, perhaps with a loved one who has died. Now it was quiet, and the town seemed on pause, or like a stage curtain waiting to be raised. As we walked, Shannon told me how she had chosen Lily Dale when looking for a project that had personal resonance. She had studied photography at Rochester Institute of Photography (RIT) for a bachelor of fine arts degree in 1998. After RIT she worked for newspapers, public relations firms, and freelance magazines. But something nagged at her. She remembered an impactful moment as a young child when her cousin had gone to Lily Dale and received a message from the spirit of their grandfather through a medium, who told her specific details of how he'd died that the medium could not have known. This memory contributed to her decision over what subjects to photograph, and she went to Lily Dale to begin taking pictures.

Lily Dale was founded in 1879 to offer a campground and meeting place for Spiritualists and was only a loose collection of groups and churches until 1893, when the National Spiritualist Association of Churches (NSAC) tried to create a denominational sensibility to organize the various communities. The camp officially became the Lily Dale Assembly in 1906. The character of the grounds indeed feels a little stuck in that time. It all has the standard features of a small town in upstate New York. There is a library, a small museum, and a post office, each of them housed in buildings built between 1880 and 1887. But here is where the likeness to a typical town ends. Lily Dale was built to create a safe place for mediums and their visitors to communicate with spirits. This, according to the NSAC, is the very definition of their religion: "Spiritualism is the Science, Philosophy, and Religion of continuous life, based upon the demonstrated fact of communication, by means of mediumship, with those who live in the Spirit World."

To this end, Lily Dale has two temples, an auditorium, a meditation garden, a "Fairy Trail," and even a pet cemetery. The museum itself offers portraits of mediums from across the years, clips from newspapers, pamphlets, and a few reproduction vintage postcards for sale. Among the highlights of the museum are "spirit paintings," which are artworks rendered by mediums in trance states, or when an image appears on a blank canvas during a séance. In one display case was an odd bit of technology: a pair of leather-and-glass goggles in a box labeled "Aura Goggles," with a card dating them to 1920. It was once thought that with a certain technological know-how, anyone could see auras using the techniques developed by Walter Kilner, which require the use of special lenses that train the eye. Kilner, a British physician in the late nineteenth century who worked with early forms of electrical medical devices, discovered that if you look through a lens or filter that has been treated with a substance called dicyanin, a blue dye made of tar, your eyes would become accustomed to perceiving certain kinds of electromagnetic radiation. Writing for the *American Freemason* magazine in 1912, the author Francis Rebman also suggests that after about three minutes, the lenses can be removed and the auras will appear. Furthermore, he maintains, after extended use, "Many people do not require the light dicyanin screen at all."

We made our way to Inspiration Stump in what are known as the Leolyn Woods, which, since the 1880s, the mediums of Lily Dale have found to be a potent area for spirit communication. Mediums will stand on the stump and receive messages twice a day during the summer season. The stump is also the favored location of orbs like the one Shannon captured with Dorothy, believed to be the energy of souls, or even guardian angels. These images, usually taken at night with a flash, show small, round, slightly transparent spheres hovering near people. The orbs are often singular, but some photos show them in blurry groups. Orb photography is a popular activity at Lily Dale, but it might be because orbs are the easiest to capture on film. There is not much mystery here, however. The slightest mote of dust on the lens will flare into an orb on the captured photo. Nevertheless, typical photos of this kind, particularly those taken at Inspiration Stump, offer a kind of gentle nudge toward imagining the reality where the souls of the departed allow themselves to be photographed. There is an innocence in these photos, in some ways contrasting with the almost fierce images of

Shannon's photographs of Lily Dale's mediums. Orb photos are easily duplicated, but what Shannon does is dependent on accident, and relies on a strange confluence of the subject, the camera, the viewer, and the spiritual expectations that are inherent in the photograph. This is clear in the photo of Dorothy with the spirit of her husband, Bob, which was not only taken in the daytime but does not render itself so easily dismissible as those displaying showers of dust flares. In Shannon's photo, Dorothy's orb is a delightful chance moment, possibly an accident of light, but also strangely ambiguous.

In another one of Shannon's photographs, a woman stands by a window, her face a range of blurred features that seem to coalesce into a mask suggesting another identity. The illusion of another entity having taken over her aspect is heightened when looking at another photo of the same woman. The medium, Sylvia Howarth, does share some commonalities with the masked version of herself—broad nose, wide forehead—but the image of her in a trance suggests that these features were utilized on behalf of the spirit, following the fundamental belief that the denizens of the hidden realms will use whatever was available to make themselves known. It's important to note that this effect is achieved technically by using a prolonged exposure in which the camera's shutter is kept open for a length of time. "Doing these time exposures means I am open to any possibility," Shannon told me. The photo of Sylvia was, as Shannon described, taken in a "mundane" situation. "[Sylvia] simply told me she was going to channel spirits for me in the light." Even with the long exposure, Shannon that wasn't expecting any kind of phenomenon to reveal itself. At the same time, Shannon admitted that using a prolonged exposure for a simple portrait of a woman standing by a window is purposely "trying to do everything wrong." Sylvia had told Shannon she would be channeling Native American spirits, and in the resulting photo, a tribal mask of sorts emerges around her face. "It truly shocked me," Shannon said when she described looking at the photo for the first time.

In her work documenting Lily Dale, Shannon isn't trying to capture photographs of spirits, or in any way attempting to prove or disprove the work of the mediums. But she quickly discovered that it was not possible to be purely objective, as a journalist would have to be. Over the years of photographing the mediums of Lily Dale, she became a participant observer, having to interpret both the experiences of mediumship and séances, as well as what the photographs manifest. It also means that as an artist, she is making conscious choices about what to reveal to the viewer.

It's a delicate balance, one fraught with potential misunderstanding both from the mediums who are her subjects and the audience of the photographs. "I'm trying to mine the mystery," Shannon explained. "I'm trying to make it as ambiguous and as confusing as possible or to have as many different interpretations as possible. I'm not trying to clarify." This might sound like deliberate trickery, something the original spirit photographers were accused of. But Shannon is not trying to deceive. The truth for her is in the ambiguity. Shannon's photographs are not intended to prove that there is life after death. The question, and the answer, are both in many ways irrelevant. A more important phenomenon is taking place, one that was also apparent in my work with Nico and her automatons. Freud makes the point in his essay "The Uncanny," which describes those frightening things that lead us back to the familiar, to what is known. He says that this titular feeling is not limited to the automaton, but "when something we have hitherto regarded as imaginary appears before us in reality, or when a symbol

takes over the full functions and significance of the thing it symbol-
izes." Because Shannon's photographs are not of literal ghosts but of
the mediums in their own state of encountering the spirits, it's as if we
are privy to the mediums' altered states of consciousness and what we
can imagine is their experience.

Describing any photograph can be difficult, but Shannon's are particularly challenging as at first glance they often look as though something in the process has indeed gone wrong. Many of her photos are of
mediums in trance states, their faces upturned toward some unseen
force or pointing downward as if they have fallen into a state of deep
hypnosis. The light is the key, though, as Shannon uses increasingly
long exposures, enlarging time so that things that are happening between the seconds are made visible. The suggestion here is that spirits
and their ilk move and act beyond what is normally perceptible, and so
by slowing down time, details not seen with the naked eye will appear,
captured by the open shutter.

Take, for example, a series of photographs of the British medium
Gordon Garforth, who describes himself on various websites as capable of something called transfiguration. This process was described as
early as 1912 in the affably titled *Spirit Mediumship: How to Develop It*.
Here, the Reverend E. W. Sprague recounts how sometimes "our spirit
friends" will change the face of the medium to look like the person who
has passed away and is being channeled. In one photo, Gordon's face
appears to be in the process of transforming as wisps of light flow around
him. A second photo shows Gordon tensing up as another figure swells
out from behind him. It is likely a double exposure, but the strain in
Gordon's body language shifts the perceived coincidence of the photo
toward something more beguiling. "Gordon said to me that he makes

ectoplasmic masks when he's in a trance, and that I will see his face change," Shannon told me. "I wasn't seeing anything like that at the time. But he does look really different in every picture."

Without a doubt, Shannon's thirty-second exposure for these photographs would account for any of the strange effects, but it's in the story of a third image where this explanation begins to dissolve. Gordon is seated, his torso pushing away from the back of the chair. His face is a blur, except for a distinct bushy mustache, which he doesn't sport in real life. The photo isn't too strange compared to others of Gordon, and Shannon herself wasn't that impressed with it within the larger body of her own work. She was also worried that it made Gordon look a little like Adolf Hitler and so was hesitant to show it to him. "But he loved it," Shannon said. He took Shannon back to his house and pulled out a yellowed and creased antique photo. It is a picture of Gordon's great-grandfather, the spirit Gordon said he was channeling, wearing the same style of thick mustache.

It is hard to tell how much seeing the photo of Gordon's great-grandfather might have changed the way I perceive the picture of Gordon in his trance state. The personas in each photograph are so strikingly similar that I can't look at Shannon's without now superimposing in my mind's eye the face of Gordon's relative. This is where technology can break down perception, creating a space whereby even the memory of how I first saw the image is forever altered by the introduction of the antique photograph into the narrative. Whether or not Gordon actually channeled his bald, mustachioed great-grandfather and was transfigured to appear like him was only realized at the moment Shannon clicked open the shutter and allowed the light and subtle movements of her subject to enlarge the actual experience. As Shannon said, nothing appeared out of the ordinary when she was taking the photos. No phantasmal mask appeared on Gordon's face. The spiritual imagination is activated afterward by the technology. It is in this sense that the Spiritualists maintained the truth of spirit photography in the face of overwhelming evidence to the contrary. The intent of the photographer is irrelevant to the spirits, who will find a way to render themselves visible.

———

Everyone at the séance was really there to see ectoplasm, the physical intrusion of the spiritual into the material. As the climactic event, it is indeed a somewhat eroticized encounter with the spirits. It is the most intimate moment for the medium. For the first time during the séance, he was exposed and vulnerable. This sexual resonance was explicitly palpable in the nineteenth century when the mediums were women, and ectoplasm was often extruded from their vaginas. Any orifice would do, of course, but this also made the woman a powerful vessel. Not only could she give birth, she could deliver a spiritual wonder into the world, often requiring the same kind of toil and strain as childbirth. It's no surprise, then, that the most famous photographer of ectoplasm was a sexologist, among his other professions as doctor and psychologist. Born in 1862, Albert von Schrenck-Notzing was a doctor who studied medicine at Munich University and eventually became interested in hypnosis. He used these techniques to help cure his patients of what were then considered sexual deviations.

It was once believed that hypnotism was a spiritual force, or "vital fluid," which in the mid-eighteenth century Franz Friedrich Anton Mesmer called "animal magnetism" and claimed it moved through and within the universe, capable of being manipulated for the purposes of healing illness. What if this "vital fluid," or some aspect of it, could be made visible? This was something Schrenck-Notzing hoped to demonstrate and began working with the medium "Eva C," a pseudonym for Marthe Béraud. Eva seemed to demonstrate extraordinary abilities beyond anything mediums had done before. The writer J. D. Beresford, in an article for the March 1922 issue of *Harper's Magazine*, claimed that Eva could even "materialize the perfect body of a tiny, nude woman, which moved all the material actions of life."

Schrenck-Notzing published *Phenomena of Materialisation: A Contribution to the Investigation of Mediumistics Teleplastics* in 1920, his complete account of working with Eva C. The book begins like many of the time related to Spiritualism with a rational apologia, explaining that science should not dismiss any claims until sufficient testing and analysis had been performed. Schrenck-Notzing writes, "Our investigation of Nature is subject to change. We have no justification for condemning *a priori*, though a healthy skepticism can only contribute to the furtherance of truth." As we saw, it was important for those early-twentieth-century investigators and Spiritualist sympathizers to be able to align their beliefs with the scientific method. Schrenck-Notzing went even further, however, asserting that mediumistic phenomena were not the result of anything supernatural, but a function of the human being's own unconscious. Schrenck-Notzing saw photography as the only legitimate means for capturing and documenting the materializations, but he also—maybe naïvely so—believed that mediums must be studied under the conditions they themselves deem necessary.

Since mediumship arose out of the Spiritualist milieu, this context, Schrenck-Notzing argued, had to be respected. Nevertheless, he still prepared to accurately photograph in a way that would prevent trickery. Schrenck-Notzing used up to nine cameras placed in various positions and various kinds of lighting. He inspected the cabinet and performed "a careful searching of [Eva's] body." His book even provides helpful diagrams of the layout of the room showing where the equipment and the sitters were situated in relation to the spirit cabinet. The result of this was that despite what he believed were strict controls over the sessions he photographed, claims of fraud began to overwhelm him. The most notorious example can be seen in two photographs, the first taken on November 27, 1912, which shows Eva from the side, a cottony materialization emanating from her mouth, and rising from behind her is another odd form with lettering on it. Another photo from May 2 the following year shows Eva C holding open the curtains of her spirit cabinet as a man's face appears on her chest. Clever investigations by Schrenck-Notzing's opponents revealed that the words seen in the first photo looked exactly like the typeface used for the magazine *Le Mirror*, and the man's head was almost exactly that of a portrait seen on the cover of the issue from April 21, 1912. Looking back at other materialization photos, it seemed obvious that despite Schrenck-Notzing's controls, he had been fooled. The photography curator Andreas Fischer writes in the essential *The Perfect Medium*, "There were many who supported this view, expressing malicious joy at the simplicity of the explanation." Schrenck-Notzing pushed the envelope of his own imagination in trying to account for the likeness of the faces to the magazine's images, going so far in his book to suggest that Eva may have indeed seen the magazine and it became the raw material that her unconscious mind used to create the materialization. He writes, "Reminiscences of former visual impressions and fragments of dream images coalesce unconsciously with the ideoplastic creations to form a unified presentation, which may be so misinterpreted as to give rise to suspicion."

Schrenck-Notzing eventually conceded, but only to say that photography simply couldn't properly capture the truth of what was seen with the naked eye during the séance. Rather than verifying the reality of materialization, the camera filtered out the experience and cast a pall of artificiality on the real. It is true that the photographs of Eva C are both absurdly fake and profoundly ambiguous. In some, the faces entangled within the ectoplasm look flat and "cut-out," and the ectoplasm itself looks like cheesecloth or cotton. In others, Eva appears to be in a deep trance state, the ectoplasm flowing out of her mouth like smoke, defying gravity. It is between these two sensibilities that the entire history of spirit photography is located: a phenomenon of some kind is being captured, and a narrative is implied that the photograph can only allude to. In the case of Eva C, there is a relationship between her and Schrenck-Notzing that is so intimate it is difficult to tell who is really the one with the most power. And power is exactly what is on display. Both are participating in an effort to provide the other with some mutual unspoken need. At the heart of magic, as we saw, is mode transcendence that is far beyond the trick or the ritual. The performance, the relationship between the magician and the audience, is one in which consciousness is altered and the world is enchanted.

As the medium prepared for what was explained by the spirit guide as an extremely perilous endeavor, I wondered about ectoplasm and why, in the cosmology of Spiritualism, spirits feel the need to present themselves in this way. Later, Shannon explained that some mediums would say it is an attempt to merge the material and spiritual worlds, which creates a healing atmosphere. The ectoplasm is merely the expression of an invisible process. The medium functions not only as a voice for the gods, but as a literal valve through which this strange spiritual substance is excreted.

For this medium in Lily Dale to produce ectoplasm, his hands had to be unbound, the curtain of the cabinet pulled aside, his gag removed, and a small candle lit in front of it. It was made clear by the spirits that they were mistrustful of the camera, despite the realm of the dead supposedly having a long history of this technology. The deep-voiced spirit then asked Shannon to take her camera from under her chair and allow it to be inspected. In complete darkness, the spirit instructed Shannon on what she would be allowed to do. She could set up her camera on a tripod, but could not use any artificial light, including the camera's flash. The only available light source would be from the candle. After everything was ready, the cabinet was opened. The medium was sitting very still, the straps that had bound his wrists now on the floor near his feet. After a moment, he started to produce a series of choking sounds until slowly a wad of a thick white substance started to emerge from his mouth. Other than the strange gurgling coming from his throat, the only other sound in the room was the clicking of the camera's shutter.

I watched through the dim candlelight as a white egg-shaped glob of matter began to extrude from the medium's mouth. He raised his hands to it and as the substance took on more mass, his fingers clutched it and began drawing it out. There seemed to be much more than could comfortably fit in the medium's cheeks, and I was reminded of a stage magician pulling multicolored scarves from their pocket. The ectoplasm was drawn and stretched like ethereal taffy from the medium's mouth. Shannon's shutter measured the time of this strange performance with each photograph, building tension until the shutter would close. Some gasped as they witnessed what they must have believed was spirit made corporeal. My attention was mostly on Shannon as she moved quietly to position herself, looking up at the medium and back to her camera, opening the shutter and then waiting for it to close. The effect of Shannon working in the room was a shift in my own experience as I tried to imagine what else she might capture that I wasn't seeing now. Was there some invisible process that might render itself in the photograph? People continued to quietly and nervously laugh, and some called out words of encouragement. I was enthralled by Shannon, however, witnessing an activity that was deeply connected to Spiritualist history. It was an attempt to insert a technological device into a process that was dependent on a human agent. Thus, there were two mediums at work here. Both had access to a special kind of truth, but what they would produce was very different.

I left Lily Dale feeling a bit let down, lamentably *unhaunted*, and without a clear sense of what mediumship means in the modern world. I had gone without expectations, and worked to leave my skepticism back in Boston. In fact, I was hoping to have a preternatural experience, to be in the presence of a medium in a trance state, and then to connect that encounter with the photographs Shannon produced. I wasn't sure how the banality of what happened would translate onto the digital image. I had felt twinges of old superstitions at Lily Dale, both hopeful and afraid that someone I had cared for deeply in this life would contact me from the other side. Alas, they had remained invisible. Or so I thought. A few days after I returned home, Shannon shared with me the photographs she had taken, and it was then I began to understand that the camera and the photograph, not the people, are the mediums through which a crossing-over had taken place.

In one photo, the medium's head seems to emerge from the darkness, his features cast in a gloom, an image that captures the dark mystery we would be encountering when he first warned us of the fraught nature of the séance. Another shows ectoplasm being drawn from the medium's mouth, a long, fluid mass stretching down toward the floor. It is a grotesque image, stranger and more surreal than I witnessed in person.

Occasionally, the photograph also reveals that which should however remain hidden. During the first half of the séance, one photo clearly shows a slide whistle on the floor, during the period Shannon could take photos. That delightfully strange noise we heard at the opening of the séance was now merely a magician's prop. This didn't reduce its effect, however. The recollection of what I felt hearing it, and later seeing the photo, revealing it as an object the medium had at hand, waged a strange battle in my consciousness. If what we were seeing was a perfectly rendered magic show dressed as a séance, an essential question at the heart of my technological quest is made evident: How much of the occult, and in the history of mediumship, was also more performance than supernatural activity? And how does technology such as the camera suggest there is yet another phenomenon outside the realm of the merely performative?

Those popular brilliant high-resolution images of quasars and nebulae are imaginary, just a bit of color added to an artist's rendition of noise and math. And yet we recognize them to be accurate in their way. Because the colorful swirls of galaxies and Magellanic clouds are rendered out of something we can't actually see, but can estimate, based on dozens of images stitched together using equations and scientific deduction, perhaps intuition. These are deliberate fabrications to facilitate our experience or understanding. Shannon's photography, on the other hand, is not manipulating the images, but instead relying on chance, accident, and glitch. Both draw a certain truth out of the abstraction of experience, like ectoplasm out of an orifice. The supernatural echoes that appear in Shannon's photos are neither true nor false, but are mirrors of a confluence of three things: the camera, the moment the photo was taken, and the viewer of the photo. As Shannon explained to me in Lily Dale, "I'm trying to play a part, but I am not trying to clarify anything."

Shannon's work is an inversion of the classical spirit photograph, particularly the ectoplasm images of Schrenck-Notzing. "He abandoned photography because it abstracted what he saw as reality," Shannon said. "He was seeing these magical things, and photography was destroying them." Photography is a special kind of looking, and can't perfectly mirror the experience of seeing. "I am embracing photography for the exact reason that Schrenck-Notzing abandoned it," Shannon explained. Schrenck-Notzing, however, could never admit to the possibility of having been deceived, instead blaming the limitations of the technology. Shannon wants to embrace the idea of deception as an area to explore.

Those working today with the séance model of mediumship often present their performance as a religious ritual, which Shannon also sees as a kind of performance art. For the mediums she's photographed, Shannon also functions as an extension of the performance. She told me during an interview later over e-mail, she sees herself as part magician: "I embrace the camera's ability to trick or fool. Crossing the boundary of what is considered unprofessional in the practice of photography—playing with motion blur, lens distortion, light leaks, flare, overexposure, and underexposure—feels magical to me."

This is not to say Shannon has not felt tricked herself, or put into a situation where any ambiguity was clearly contrived. But this kind of trickery is not necessarily deceitful. Today, there is a subculture in which the medium we sat with is a part, that is trying to bring back the

Victorian-era séance, with its dramatic effects: floating trumpets, dramatic and startling sounds like banging and otherworldly shrieks, and, of course, ectoplasm. It is small, to be sure, but there is a desire to bring drama—performance—back to the séance. What I experienced in the room with the medium existed, as we saw, within a tradition of stage magic where the medium or magician was bound inside a closed cabinet and then a series of "supernatural" phenomena occurred, including the sounds of horns and timpani, and sometimes spirit forms would seem to appear in the darkness. Just as the stage magician would use these selfsame techniques to debunk Spiritualism, the character of the magician and the medium were once so blurred it was impossible to tell what kind of performance was taking place.

None of my time at Lily Dale or at the séance led me to believe that spirits of the dead communicate with the living, or that ectoplasm is an actual substance that tethers the two worlds. And working with Shannon and studying her photographs did not convince me, either. What was revealed to me is that my own consciousness can endure interior liminal spaces. Furthermore, Shannon's photographs—and indeed some elements of spirit photography overall—act to expand my imagination. How far, I wondered, could I let myself go into that realm? And how far had others gone to prove that the dead never really die, that the soul is not bound to the body?

Friedrich Jürgenson in his studio in Höör, Sweden, around 1985

CHAPTER 5

Guided by Voices

The microphone is heavy and plugs into the reel-to-reel recorder with a curious pin arrangement that I have never seen before or since. The recorder is a Uher 4000, part of an assortment of audiovisual equipment my father, Byron, had used when I was a kid in the 1960s and '70s. The Uher synchronized sound with his French-made Beaulieu Super 8 movie camera, and he edited the results with his Atlas Warner editor and Bolex splicer. My family would watch the completed films on a Bell & Howell projector set up in the den. While the camera and its related equipment were interesting to me, it was the reel-to-reel that I would ask to borrow as a kid. Unlike my cassette recorder, the exposed tape of the Uher was like something from an espionage movie, and threading the tape through the heads made me feel like an audio engineer. The unit had four speeds, so whatever I recorded could be sped up or slowed down to giddy excess. I made tapes filled with stories of orcs and elves with the background music of Rush's *A Farewell to Kings*. I sang in broken falsetto to Queen and Alice Cooper.

I still have that reel-to-reel player now, one of the few treasures I retrieved from my late father's house.

This tape recorder was haunting the edges of my time spent talking to Donna Hogan, an independent researcher and practitioner in what is known as electronic voice phenomena or EVP (also called instrumental transcommunication or ITC), a belief that spirits of the dead, or other otherworldly beings, can communicate with the living using various forms of electronic equipment. Donna was born in 1965 in what she described as "badly scarred" Liverpool, England, which was still recovering from World War II, and her childhood was, she recalled, "spent playing on derelict bomb sites." She is not who I expected, to be honest. Donna is a mother and grandmother, and cares full-time for her youngest daughter, who is autistic. Her upbringing was in a large and chaotic, predominantly Irish Catholic home, but she does not call herself a religious person and doesn't follow any faith tradition. During our very first video chat, Donna had suggested I use my father's tape recorder to experiment with EVP. She was excited about the possibilities, but I was hesitant. I wanted to learn more, understand not only the process but the techniques and the intentions behind seeking voices of the dead.

During our talk, Donna explained to me the moment ITC/EVP changed her life. It was portended by what she described as a series of dreamlike premonitions. She was close to her sister's husband Neil, and in the late summer of 2005, whenever she would see him, the image of a traffic police officer would arise in her mind. Along with the image came a feeling of doom. "In the UK, if a traffic police officer comes to your home, you know that something really bad has happened," she told me. The images were so real, so wrought with a sense of déjà vu, that she told a few relatives that she felt an imminent danger, and around Neil in particular. That September, Neil was in a road accident and was instantly killed.

Donna recounted the trauma of that day, but it wasn't until the family went to the mortuary that the "phenomena," as she called it, began. Donna and her relatives had been told to turn off their cell phones so as not to disturb others in the mortuary who were identifying their deceased loved ones. "As soon as we walked into the room where my brother-in-law was laid out, my mobile phone turned on," Donna said. "And I'll never forget it, because my sister quite oddly just turned to me and said, 'That's probably Neil.'" At the time, Donna thought her sister was making a dark joke, or not thinking straight given her obvious distress. But after they exited the morgue, the whole entourage—Donna, her sister, her partner, and a police officer—all began experiencing trouble with their phones. One phone wouldn't turn on and ultimately had to be replaced. Donna had dozens of empty text messages from an unknown number. "But because someone had just died in the family, I didn't even have time to think of how odd that was," Donna told me.

Donna stayed with her grieving sister for two weeks. It was when she returned to her own home that her life turned upside down. "I was raised Catholic, but don't go to church, and had no interest in the paranormal or anything like that," she said. That day back at her house, her relationship to supernatural ideas would dramatically change. It began by simply listening to the messages on her answering service. The first message sounded like a fuzzy electrical noise. "There was a pause, then a male voice. I'll never forget the voice. It was my brother-in-law's voice saying, 'Hello, is Donna there? It's Neil.'" Then more static, and another voice broke through saying, "Hello? Are you there? Gosh, I think I've just had a crossed line." Donna played that message repeatedly to be sure that she was identifying the voice correctly. "I wasn't frightened. It just unnerved me," she recalled.

The time and date on the message were from four days after Neil was killed, so Donna wanted to know if her voice mail—a digital system provided by her phone company, British Telecom, had somehow time-stamped the message incorrectly. "I phoned and asked to speak to an engineer," Donna recalled. "And I said, 'The time and the dates on my answer phone system [are] incorrect.' And he laughed at me and said, 'Well, that's actually impossible, because our network service is linked up to the Greenwich Mean Time clock.'" The engineer went on to explain that for a call to be time-stamped incorrectly the entire network would have to have failed, and, as he told Donna, "There hadn't been a network failure for many, many years." The date and time, he told her, were accurate. Donna explained the crossed line message, but when the engineer began to sound impatient with her, she told him the voice of the man whose message is recorded on the answering system died three days before the message came in." Donna told me the line went very quiet for a brief period and then she heard him take a deep breath. The technician then told Donna something she said changed her life: "He actually said to me, 'Look, I know this is going to sound crazy, but it's not the first time I've heard about this phenomenon, and it probably won't be the last. The only thing I can say to you as a bit of advice is to Google 'phone calls from the dead.'"

Donna discovered an enormous amount of material on the Internet of people claiming to have received phone calls from dead loved ones, but she was still convinced that the message from her brother-in-law was a network glitch. A forensic report during the investigation into the fatal crash showed that he hadn't called Donna on his phone to her home phone for over two weeks before he died. "He was always getting himself into lots of scrapes and stuff," Donna told me, "and once he said to me, 'If I ever get myself into any trouble that I can't really get myself out of or that may upset your sister, do you think I'd be able to ring you?'" Donna has since come to believe that when a person has died suddenly or traumatically, the desire for closure—to say goodbye to loved ones—is so strong that their consciousness can leak out into the physical world. "He did what he had asked to do while alive," Donna explained. "He was in trouble and tried to ring me up."

Six months after the tragic death of her brother-in-law, Donna received a phone call from her mother asking her to come visit. She told Donna there was something she wanted her to listen to. Her mother said, "I've got one of those voices." Donna's mother is the secretary of her local credit union. Part of her duties are to record the meetings and then transcribe and disseminate them. She sat in on all the meetings, taped them, took them home, and typed everything up using headphones. While she was transcribing, her doorbell rang, and instead of stopping the tape, she pressed "record" by accident. The friend at the door was there to pick her up for bingo, so she left the house, with her husband at home. The next day, she was infuriated when she realized she had taped over the meeting minutes, but listened to the whole tape hoping she hadn't lost all of it. At one point, the recorder picked up the voice of her husband—who had been suffering from prostate cancer—and she heard him talking to the family dog, saying, "Oh, I wish this pain would go away." And then she heard a clearly female voice with a thick Dublin accent say, "Poor, sweet Willy." When she played the tape for Donna, she immediately recognized the voice as her aunt Kathleen, who had passed away twelve years ago. This recorded voice phenomenon and the voice mail message from her brother-in-law would set Donna on her long journey into investigating EVPs. For the first twelve months, she admittedly didn't document all her experiences or keep the recordings, so unfortunately the original incidences were not available for me to listen to.

Donna described her work with EVP like being on a beach, "waiting for the wave so I can surf." Over the years, Donna has observed the methods for recording EVP changing drastically. And even though anyone can download an EVP application for their cell phone or computer, there is still no consensus, even among seasoned practitioners, as to what the voices really are. Donna noted that many people are drawn to EVP research because they've lost a loved one and are seeking contact or answers. Some researchers take a particularly religious view, identifying voices in the static as those from guardian angels. Others see EVP as evidence of life after death. When I asked Donna, who does not consider herself a Spiritualist, if she believes in life after death, she said, "I believe in consciousness after death." The voice of Donna's brother-in-law did not arise out of life as we know it, Donna explained. "How bloody frustrating would it be if you wanted to communicate to someone to explain what's going happening on the other side and you don't have a voice box?" The spirits, Donna explained, would try to utilize any means to get a message to the living. "If consciousness survives, then somehow it imprints," she told me.

Some practitioners believe EVPs are voices from extraterrestrials or interdimensional entities that operate on frequencies beyond the human capacity to hear but whose goings-on can sometimes be picked up by electronic equipment. YouTube videos offer EVPs of angelic choirs, alien transmissions from beings called Archons inadvertently picked up by NASA, and even the voice of the deceased actor Robin Williams. For the most part, most EVP researchers believe the voices once belonged to living human beings who have died. Whether it is their souls crying out from purgatory or a friendly higher consciousness offering advice or greetings is still up for debate. Some EVP investigators believe that the technology is the essential link between this physical world and the realm of the spirit. Perhaps it was that historically, without an electronic agent, the spirits were left to the old methods—speaking through a human medium, or signaling their presence via a Ouija board, for example—but none of that could be verified in the way the EVP community believes is possible with their techniques. Because they are born of scientific research and engineering with a rational and methodological foundation, modern technologies used for EVP lend themselves to an audience or community who subscribe to the historical cultural tendency toward the empirical. Electronic equipment—a tape recorder or a smartphone app—provides the modern-day spirit a means to cross over that works with how we understand the modern-day world around us. EVP exists within a context of the rational, of natural laws and forces of physics. A century ago, we had only table rappers or voice throwers. Today in the EVP community, technology is both a literal and symbolic method for spirit communication and acts as a tool that can aid in EVP being understood as not only rational but quantifiable. Spiritualism, where most contemporary notions of spirit communication have their origins, was where the belief in spirit communication was first grounded in scientific concepts and discoveries. Using technology is merely an extension of that belief.

The New York–based Spiritualist newspaper *The Spiritual Telegraph*, published between 1852 and 1860, was so named after the very term used to describe mediums: "spiritual telegraphs." As demonstrated in the history of spirit photography, mediumship and other forms of spirit communication, such as table tipping, were aligned with contemporary scientific ideas. The invention of the telegraph—the ability to communicate over great distances without wires—could not have been more perfectly timed for its use as both a metaphor for the medium and as a comparative *scientific* process. This gave the work of spiritual mediums a kind of legitimacy when framed as rational and measurable. It was even suggested that the science utilized by spirits might be even greater than that wrought by human beings. One letter writer to *The Spiritual Telegraph* related how their medium friends communicated with each other by way of spirits delivering messages back and forth; that they "can see no reason why we should not invoke the aid of Spirits in establishing a spiritual telegraph, which would supersede the necessity of the magnetic telegraph now used, and be less expensive." Historian Bret E. Carroll notes that mediums saw themselves as another kind of apparatus, one that was guided by spirits, but still acting on the same physical laws that allowed wireless communication to be possible. The telegraph, whether in the form of a physical or spiritual communication device, is a kind of technology, just as it was believed that "Spiritualism itself," Carroll writes, was "an extension of science." It wasn't until the next century that the metaphor would invert. Instead of spiritual telegraphs functioning in the way of, if not better than, the magnetic telegraph, then radios and other methods of receiving electromagnetic signals might be the true medium with which to speak to the dead. Eventually, however, that medium could be replaced completely by technology believed to be sensitive enough to capture the voices of spirits as they hitched a ride along electromagnetic waves.

The premiere issue of *The Unexplained: Mysteries of Mind Space & Time*, published in 1980 by Orbis Publishing in the United Kingdom, included a curious seven-inch record called a flexi disc, an audio record cut on very thin, flexible vinyl that could be easily inserted into a magazine. The flexi disc was titled *Breakthrough: An Amazing Experiment in Electronic Communication with the Dead*. The recording is a repressing of a 1971 release, a primer to the work of the Latvian psychologist Konstantin Raudive, who that year published an English-language translation of his 1968 book, titled *Breakthrough*. The book is essentially a series of transcripts of the tens of thousands of voices Raudive recorded in the mid-1960s using various devices such as a simple tape recorder, an untuned radio, and a small crystal radio—called a catwhisker—of what in the book he claims are "psychical-spiritual" beings. Over e-mail, Peter Brookesmith, the former editor of *The Unexplained*, told me he became aware of EVP from reading deeply on the paranormal as he and his colleagues were laying out the magazine, but that spirit communication via electronic gadgets wasn't what people were talking about yet. The staff of *The Unexplained* were editors by profession. Peter had previously edited a children's encyclopedia, a wildlife encyclopedia, and a history of railways. When it came to the subject of the supernatural, Peter was not well versed and recalls having to just go in deep, learn everything he could, and then talk to the experts. Having secured the rights to repress the Raudive records as a flexi disc influenced the magazine's editorial and marketing decisions. "I don't believe people were talking much about spontaneous human combustion, either, but it's intrinsically such a weird notion that it was irresistible."

In the introduction to *Breakthrough*, Raudive wastes no time setting up his position. He writes, "Tape-recorder, radio, and microphone give us facts in an entirely impersonal way and their objectivity cannot be challenged." Raudive's techniques and theories have become the basis for the entire EVP culture, but where many experimenters frame their experiences in religious terms, Raudive took a decidedly spiritual-psychological approach, positing that the voices we hear are not souls trapped between heaven and hell, but "overselves" that exist within a "transcendental reality." Raudive was inspired to begin his own experiments after reading about those of Friedrich Jürgenson, who detailed his own experiences in the 1959 book *Voices from Space*.

Jürgenson had first heard voices when he listened to birdsong he recorded at his parents' home in Sweden. The birdsong was ultimately drowned out by the hiss of the motor in the recording device, but in the background the voice of a Norwegian man could be detected, and as far as Jürgenson knew, there was no one nearby whose voice would have been picked up by the microphone. Later, Jürgenson tried again to record the birds, and this time on listening to the tape he heard the unmistakable voice of his deceased mother calling out to him: "When I listen through the tape, a voice was heard to say 'Friedel, can you hear me? It's mammy . . .' It was my dead mother's voice. 'Friedel' was her special nickname for me." At the time, Jürgenson was an artist, but the moment crystalized his life's work. He was determined to understand what he called "mystical connections . . . floating in the ether." For the next dozen or so years, Jürgenson amassed hundreds of tapes of recorded voices, many recorded from radio frequencies between 1445 and 1500 kHz, after a spirit voice told him to "use the radio."

In 2000, the British sound art collective Ash International exhibited Jürgenson's collection in Stockholm, Sweden, in a show called "Friedrich Jürgenson from the Studio for Audioscopic Research." The related CD is long out of print, but the composer and artist Carl Michael von Hausswolff, who acts as archivist of the Friedrich Jürgenson estate, provided me with MP3s. Some of the recordings are simple, a voice rising out of crackly static or strains of music. Others are more suggestive.

Two of the recordings are said to be from the theosophist Annie Besant, who says in German, as translated in the liner notes, "Freddie we're peeping—the Dead—we sit on the deathship . . . the Dead sit with us." A few are the stuff of nightmares. A voice sings a loose, haunting version of "Hava Nagila," and alongside, another voice says, "Bojevski—Jürgenson," as if to tell Jürgenson who is singing. The liner notes confirm that Gleb Bojevski was a deceased friend of Jürgenson. But it's the recording itself that is unnerving. The song is so out of context, buried under the noise of fuzz and clicks, as if Jürgenson had picked up someone who didn't know they were being recorded. Being uncertain of what you are hearing is disconcerting. I don't believe they are the voices of ghosts or spirits, but why do I have to keep reminding myself of that when listening to them? We expect the physical world to be stable, to behave and obey certain laws. If these do not hold true, if they can be broken, rearranged, what other laws of physics as we know them may be elastic?

Like the Jürgenson material, the Raudive flexi disc included in the magazine is an auditory uncanny valley, working along the same psychospiritual spectrum as automata. It opens with a man's voice explaining, "The text spoken by the voices and the sound volume are exactly the same as in the original recording. To help the ear adapt to the strange rhythm, rapidity, and softness of the voice entities' speech, each utterance is repeated several times." A woman's voice—credited on the sleeve as Nadia Fowler—introduces each track with some explanatory context when needed. The first voice is said to be that of Margarete Petrautzki, a friend of Raudive's who did not believe in life after death. After she died, Raudive tried to communicate with her and asked how she felt in the beyond. The response, in German, is presented by Nadia before we hear it: *Denker, ich bin*," or in English, "Imagine, I am."

Without Nadia's interpreting the voice it would be hard to make out what is being said, but after listening to the record and the dozens of examples presented, a strange uncertainty begins to form. Certainly, these could all be fake, and despite the claims in the book that they were recorded under strict controls, there is no reason to believe there are any unexplainable phenomena at play. But the voices are so strange, so deeply ambiguous, that it begins to feel as though they might be real after all. This is where all good EVP recordings reside. If the voices on the record were perfectly clear and understandable, they would, oddly enough, seem completely fake. The voices Raudive captured are eerie, and if faked are ingeniously produced. It must have been a deliberate effort to create the most disconcerting experience when listening to them.

There are a few earlier examples often mentioned in literature about EVP, but information on them is scant. The most interesting is the tale of the Russian anthropologist Vladimir Bogoraz, who between 1899 and 1901 studied and lived with the Chukchee tribe on the Chukchee Peninsula bordering the Bering Sea. In Bogoraz's memoir of living with the tribe, he recounts how much of their folklore and ritual practices involve supernatural entities called *ke'let*, some of which are helpful while others are malevolent. During one ceremony, the spirits possessed the shamans and spoke through them, which is referred to as "separate voices." Bogoraz writes, "Some voices are at first faint, as if coming from afar; as they gradually approach, they increase in volume, and at last they rush into the room, pass through and out, decreasing, and dying away in the remote distance." Sometimes the voices are the sounds of animals and insects, words in a foreign tongue, and a voice imitation of clapping hands. Bogoraz heard a spirit whisper in his ear, and another voice from the ground between his legs, while the shaman appeared to be in a complete trance as he played a drum.

At one point, Bogoraz set up a gramophone to record the "separate voices" inside a tent with the shaman sitting far from the microphone, which was then a cone or funnel. After listening to the recordings, he wrote: "The records show a very marked difference between the voice of the shaman himself, which sounds from afar, and the voices of the 'spirits,' who seemed to be talking directly into the funnel." This empirical anthropological record, published by the American Museum of Natural History, is understood by many EVP researchers to be proof of the first examples of recorded spirit voices. Some claim the recordings don't exist anymore; others say they are continually studied with no explanation forthcoming of how the spirit voices are produced. What the EVP community fails to acknowledge is what Bogoraz himself said about the voices: "The Chukchee ventriloquists display great skill, and could with credit to themselves carry on a contest with the best artists of the kind of civilized countries." It's easy to overlook Bogoraz's interpretation here, despite his accounts of bearing witness to the ceremonies. The only rational explanation would be that ventriloquism was used, but even Bogoraz admits that "the performance of the shaman far transcends anything attainable by a person of ordinary powers."

In 1980, the phenomenon known as EVP was still largely unheard of. Mediumship, ESP, near-death experiences, and UFOs, however, were at the center of a trending storm of interest in the paranormal and the occult, but the idea that we could listen to the dead via electronic equipment had not yet reached the popular imagination until this issue of *The Unexplained*. In the United States, audiences were introduced to the idea in the 1981 *In Search Of* episode "Spirit Voices" in which the researcher D. Scott Rogo, coauthor with Raymond Bayless of *Phone Calls from the Dead* (1979), suggests that attempts to communicate with spirts via electronic devices such as telephones and tape recorders are likely the result of "active experimentation on the other side to make contact with the living." Other visionaries were working in their basements and garages hoping to come up with the device or method that would best offer more than those clipped, interrupted voices breaking through a haze of auditory static.

The April 7, 1982, issue of the *Harrisburg Daily Register* offered the headline "'Dial-the-Dead' TV Coming Soon, Researcher Insists," with an accompanying article detailing a press conference held by George Meek, then a seventy-one-year-old retired engineer who had built a device he called the Spiricom, with instruction from the spirit of a dead physics teacher named George Jeffries Mueller. While he didn't demonstrate Spiricom to the reporters, he played tapes that included recordings of him and Mueller, as well as Meek's partner, William O'Neil, discussing how to build the machine. The Spiricom is not a single instrument but a configuration made up of a signal generator transmitted over a radio frequency, picked up by a receiver and then recorded. Meek had developed an entire cosmology of how and why he believed communication with spirits was possible, which involved a complicated mapping of planes of existence that vibrate at different frequencies. With sensitive enough equipment, we can interact with them, he claimed. The Spiricom recordings are decidedly different from other EVP examples. Those of Jürgenson and Raudive are sometimes hard to discern, but they are clearly human. The Spiricom voices sound electronic, as if the entity must construct a voice out of the electromagnetic *stuff* they are accessing in order to speak. This lends a kind of authenticity to Meek's efforts. Why would disembodied spirits sound like themselves when alive? Within the EVP schema, the synthetic voices of the Spiricom are consistent with the perennial idea that spirits must use whatever means available to break through to our side.

Computer software developments have again changed the practice of EVP investigations. There is no real consensus in the EVP community over how to frame the phenomena revealed via software and applications. At the time of this writing, there were over sixty different EVP-related iPhone and Android apps, each with a markedly different sensibility. Some were presented as scientific devices, others as nightmarish encounters with dark entities. For $19.95, I purchased a Windows-based program called Ethereal. The user interface offers several control options, such as the ability to transmit messages into the spirit world by typing questions or other entreaties into a text field and pressing the "Send Message" button. Other controls include volume settings for both the output of voices as well as preprogrammed music—a kind of new age pastiche of airy angelic sound effects that are intended to offer comfort to the spirits. The software can also connect to Bluetooth to scan those frequencies directly. Like many EVP applications, it is described as needing to be learned by the spirits, so that over time communications will improve. Using the software a few times, the basic functions involved an array of recorded voices chopped up and randomized. As with other EVP devices, the idea is to give the spirits raw material to work with. But rather than using a string of simple words, the developers chose words that are inherently spiritual, such as "angel," "love," "mother," "child," and "blessed," spoken by a reassuring British-sounding male voice or a wistful female. As such, every session included an output of messages that contained these words.

The developer of the application, Anthony Sanchez, explained to me in detail how Ethereal works. Working from the belief that spirits need raw data with which to manipulate words, Anthony created his own version of an application known as EVPmaker, a piece of software that takes any bit of audio—such as the recording of a radio talk show—and cuts it into smaller bits, generating a randomized mash-up of the original. Many EVP researchers use a voice synthesizer's phonemes—the unique sounds that make up any given language. The phoneme file is loaded into EVPmaker, and the output is a string that can be used by the sprits to construct words, a technology I imagine Raudive would have loved. Using EVPmaker, Anthony creates a very large master file of raw noise. This unprocessed sound is mixed with content Anthony writes, which is then converted from text to speech in one of the two voices described earlier. Anthony then uses Bluetooth to scan UHF frequencies, which he explained do not carry any transmitted songs, voices, or other clear chatter. Ethereal then looks for patterns in the UHF bands and when it finds something, assigns it to one of the audio files that is created by EVPmaker running in the background.

My results varied, but not one of the sessions offered anything in the way of a clear answer to a direct question, nor did I recognize any names of people, places, or ideas that were personal to me or had some meaning in the moment. I was always bothered by the intrusion of those categorically "spiritual" words that were preloaded into the audio file. I wondered if, as with Shannon's photographs, listening to EVP recordings made by someone I trusted, with context and narrative, might provoke my imagination and allow me to hear in a new way.

Part of what was necessary here was faith. I believed what Donna said about the conditions in which her recordings were made. Without that trust, the EVPs might sound like a glitch in the device, an electronic artifact or stray noise that Donna simply didn't register at the time. In one of Donna's early EVP recordings, for example, she is in the bathtub, and splashes of water can be heard. It seems odd that one would attempt to record entities while in the bath, but Donna explained to me that many researchers have found that the sound of running water can enhance the possibility of paranormal events. The origins of this belief are sketchy, but likely to originate in the idea that water is electrically conductive, and so provides spirits with a "stream" through which to swim into our world. In the recording, Donna is washing her face with a cosmetic wipe and then tosses it into the toilet. You can hear her voice clearly say, "Yay! Goal!" Followed by another, quieter voice, saying, "Got it in the toilet." Donna told me she was alone in the house, with no TV or radio on. The moment is so prosaic, my first thought was that maybe it's her own consciousness externalized, or that she simply didn't realize she was speaking out loud. The second voice is distinct, but what is stranger is that it occurs so quickly after Donna speaks, almost overlapping. The second voice is too close in time to Donna's own to be edited out or isolated, in order to be heard as distinct from hers. In another recording, Donna was alone at a friend's house and caught a series of otherworldly burbles, like something from a horror science fiction film. It is unnerving and was the first EVP I'd heard that sounded ominous, as if something not of this world had broken through.

In both cases, technology is not simply the proof—in the form of the recording—but the essential means through which the entity makes itself known. Donna didn't hear the voices occur at the time, which is why these are EVP and not recordings of paranormal or supernatural phenomena being witnessed in the moment. The voices are "electronic" because they are dependent on the device to become realized. In another recording, Donna can be heard fiddling with the recorder when a barely audible male voice, sounding almost irritated, says, "Stupid." Again, this is easily read as a reflection or reverberation of her own internal subconscious. It is a bizarre moment, and the voice has a sinister quality that lends itself to the creepier elements of EVP. We are, at least in theory, talking about voices from the dead, an idea that sits at the heart of fears of the supernatural. Death is the one mystery we are supposed to leave alone, something religions and pop culture have long agreed on.

The metaphor of technology as a medium is almost too spot-on, but this doesn't undermine how perfectly it describes exactly how things like EVP are simply extensions of ancient magical practices. We have been listening for spirits with strange devices for centuries. Necromancy—the art of communicating with the dead—was considered one of the darkest forms of magical practice. Many Bible passages warn against any person who "inquires of the dead." The Torah is particularly worried about the Hebrew people participating in necromantic rites that belong to other nations. The New Testament offers a more cautionary approach, where in 1 John 4:1, the apostle teaches that some spirits are good, but some are not to be trusted. And then there is poor starving Lazarus, whom Jesus raises from the dead. The most curious case of spirit communication in the Bible is found in the first book of Samuel. After the death of Samuel, Saul exiled any necromancers who might be living in Israel, worried they would try to wrest secrets from Samuel's spirit. But Saul begins to worry about the Philistine army at his gates. Disguised, he goes in search of the Witch of Endor, a medium who can speak to the dead. Some translations and interpretations of this story explain that the witch used a talisman, a tool of sorts needed to raise the spirit of Samuel. She conjures Samuel's spirit, who essentially tells Saul the unwelcome news that the war will go badly.

The requirement of some instrument or mechanism to function as an extension of the medium's gift gives rise to the use of technology for supernatural purposes, particularly as it relates to communicating with the dead or other spirits. This is where EVP intersects with the ancient occult practice of divination. Divination almost always requires an implement through which the divine (or infernal) spirits can speak. The earliest forms of divination likely used animal entrails (known as haruspicy) and bones. Tibetan Buddhists have used Mo, a form of dice divination to make choices in a particular situation. By tossing the dice, the outcome is determined by the spirit of the bodhisattva (an enlightened saint) Manjushri, whose answer will suggest a course of action. Like necromancy, throwing lots in the form of stones or pebbles is often mentioned in the Bible as a way of making important decisions or dividing property. In the randomness, divine or supernatural influence can be made to operate. The use of lots presents a material focus or medium for the diviner, and even though the outcome is random, it is directed by an invisible agency. We've all drawn lots in a game of some kind or pulled the short straw to see who goes first (or last), and while we might not always like the outcome, there is a sense of fairness as the result seems somehow fated, out of our hands to argue with, a decision made by forces greater than us.

Often, divination wasn't based on sortilege or randomness, but on special devices. Tarot cards contain four suits and twenty-two trumps (Fortune, the Magician, the Lovers, etc.), each having specific symbolic meaning. The cards function as archetypes and are believed to correspond to various spiritual attributes. But tarot cards are also dependent on some element of chance, as the cards are shuffled before the medium or fortune-teller deals them out. Other divination objects are used more deliberately and rely on a certain sensitivity in the person making use of them. Dowsers use specially shaped metal or wooden rods to find treasure or sources of water, but often to speak with spirits. The dowser asks a question, and the spirits are thought to move the rod in a way that can be construed as "yes" or "no" answers. A variation on the use of a rod is the pendulum, whereby a heavy stone with a pointed end is suspended by a thread or string and the directions of its revolutions can be read as an affirmative or negative response to a query, such as the sex of a baby when held over a pregnant woman's belly.

The most ubiquitous divinatory apparatus—the Ouija board, made by the Parker Brothers game company—is found in households all over the country. First patented in 1891, the sturdy wooden board adorned with letters, numbers, and the whimsical "GOOD BYE," and its familiar three-legged planchette, the Ouija has since been packaged as a game and produced by Parker Brothers in the millions. As author Mitch Horowitz points out in his book *Occult America*, Spiritualists had been using homemade "talking boards" starting in the late 1850s, when there were numerous related devices. While all forms of divination have been accused at one time or another of being tools of the devil, the Ouija has long had a perceived air of malevolence around it. In a sort of collective superstition, the odd movement of the planchette sliding across the board feels ominous as if moved by some diabolical hand. It didn't help that the Ouija board is featured in the 1973 movie *The Exorcist*, certainly one of the most frightening films of my generation. In the movie, the board is used by the devil to communicate with the still innocent and uninhabited character of the child Regan, who will soon become possessed by him. The Ouija here prefigures a 360-degree head turn and a bout of explosive green vomit.

Despite the diabolic undertones that have attached themselves to the board, other Ouija-like games appeared, such as the 1967 poorly named ka-bala, a fortune-telling toy that used a black marble that rolled along a track and landed in various positions. The Finger of Fate from 1971 was a circular board housed in plastic that used a magnet to suspend a ball above a certain printed letter or number. In all these, the functionary element is that of a mechanism or instrument that makes it possible for the spirit world to interact with us.

One afternoon I received an e-mail from Donna and was surprised to see a photo attached—a still image of moving water—as opposed to the audio files she had been sharing. The surface is shimmering with light, and superimposed on the water are small white squiggles and numbers. The image, Donna told me, was captured by videotaping water, in this case. This form of ITC extends back directly to the technique of scrying with mirrors, glass, and water, and other divination methods, such as the use of mirrors, crystals, or other polished stones. There is a curious collection in the British Museum of stones and crystals belonging to the astrologer and mathematician John Dee, who in 1583 with his companion Edward Kelley, used them to learn Enochian, the secret language of angels, said to have once been spoken by Adam in Eden to name the animals. Through these stones, Dee claimed he and Kelley spoke to the angel Uriel. Dee asked the questions and Kelley, the "scryer," looked into the stones for messages and heard voices emanating from them.

In his writing, Dee details numerous conversations with loquacious angels who talked to him through his "shew stones"—one of which Dee describes as "big as an egg: most bright, clear, and gorgeous"—and scrying mirrors—called speculum—via his companion and medium Kelley. (Their complicated relationship is the stuff of scandal—such as a night of wife swapping—and their subsequent influence on the history of magic is profound, but not within the scope of this book.) Dee's stones were necessary mechanisms for his interaction with spirits. Dee writes that the stone is the device that can do what the human ear cannot. An angel calling itself Nalvage confirms this for him: "As the ear is the chief sense; so, being infected, it is the greatest hindrance. Many there be that thrust themselves between you and me: and they are increased. Power is given again to the Shew Stone; and thou shalt not be hindered." Here again is the origin of the EVP conception that supernatural entities are not that capable of speaking to us without a mediating instrument. Often, these are crafted items.

Scrying with crystals and mirrors was also used for more mundane affairs. In 1566, the British explorer Sir Humphrey Gilbert—half brother to Sir Walter Raleigh—had just returned from fighting in Ireland and had his eyes on exploring the Northwest Passage. Queen Elizabeth instead sent him back to Ireland, but during his brief time in England he seemed to be looking for support for his dream of finding the westward route from the Atlantic to the Pacific Oceans. His inquiries were not to wealthy patrons, but to the spirits of King Solomon, Job, and the demons Assessel (also called Azazel) and Oriens, among other denizens of the netherworld, using an obsidian mirror and a flat piece of polished crystal. The products of the expressions of the human hand are a necessary part of what makes the communication possible, even if simply a stone polished and cut to precise dimensions.

As in the previous story of the Witch of Endor, there are a number of other mentions in the Bible of a mysterious object called Urim, often named along with its counterpart Thummim. These puzzling references will take a definitive form when on August 4, 2015, at a news conference in Salt Lake City, the Church of Jesus Christ of Latter-day Saints revealed photos of an egg-shaped, striated brown stone, the very same type—the church spokesperson explained—that was supposedly used by Joseph Smith to translate the golden tablets that would come to be known as the Book of Mormon. Smith had originally used this "seer stone" to hunt for treasure. Most accounts describe Smith putting the stones into his hat and pressing his face against them to block out any light. The greatest treasure was yet to be found, however. One evening the angel Moroni came to Smith in a vision that led him to a treasure cache containing the golden tablets. The Mormon scholar D. Michael Quinn illuminates this story in his masterful work *Early Mormonism and the Magic World View*, explaining that in American folk magic traditions, it was often believed that spirits haunted the locations of buried treasure, often riches they had hidden during their lifetime. But Moroni's treasure contained something else: a special tool needed to read the plates. As Smith writes in his own account:

Also, that there were two stones in silver bows—and these stones, fastened to a breastplate, constituted what is called the Urim and Thummim—deposited with the plates; and the possession and use of these stones were what constituted "seers" in ancient or former times; and that God had prepared them for the purpose of translating the book.

The stones Urim and Thummim call back to those named in the Hebrew Bible as belonging to, and set into, a breastplate to be used as a method of prophecy. While Smith's stones were supposedly discovered in 1823, his mother Lucy would give them a bit of contemporary dress.

In some accounts, Lucy describes the use of the stones as being like spectacles or eyeglasses, attached to the breastplate. The Mormon writer Ogden Kraut went so far as to say that "a seer stone, or Urim and Thummim, would perform as a miniature television set. The difference of the control being directed to the will of the seer who can look into the past, the present, or even into the future."

The desire to link ancient forms of magic to technology is, of course, to give modern meaning to the object, but this tendency also suggests that technology is a functional metaphor for magic no matter how mutually opposed the two would seem. Rational categories as they are normally applied don't work here. The rational is embedded in the material aspects of the device, be it a planchette, a stone, or a tape recorder. These ground the divinatory experience in the actual—physical—world, which lends them a realness, removing doubt. And when spirits want to reach us they are bound by the same laws, even though they are using those laws in ways that science would say are simply not possible. EVP offers a window into that odd disconnect between technology and science. Yet software like EVPmaker is the result of the scientific process. A tape recorder, no matter what it is used to record, only works because of the long days and hours of testing certain hypotheses that are repeatable, so that the manufacturers of something like my Uher 4000 could be certain every unit coming off the line would function as the next, as intended. The devices work because of what we know about magnetic fields and the properties of ferric oxide. But when I attempt to use the Uher to capture sounds of disembodied souls, I have to pull away from the science that makes the act even possible. There is nothing in scientific literature or documented repeatable experiments that confirm spirits exist and can communicate along electromagnetic frequencies. I hold fast to the science that allows me to use a piece of equipment like a vintage reel-to-reel tape recorder, but I must put aside scientific rationalism once I press the "record" button in the hope of hearing spirits.

In his essential study of EVP titled *Rorschach Audio*, the sound artist Joe Banks explains that the use of technology to listen for voices between worlds deepens what he argues is an auditory illusion by creating a visual illusion: "The illusion in question is that, in making use of technological products of scientific research . . . EVP research setups superficially resemble scientific experiments." Banks shows how various forms of "auditory projection," or what he refers to as sound illusions in which "the mind projects meaning into ambiguous, indistinct, and incomplete imagery," consist mostly of stray radio transmissions from the incredible array of electronic devices that populate our world. Our brains then edit, rearrange, and sometimes insert words where they might not have been. We also delete and ignore what feels irrelevant or contains a message we are unable to hear. With my own experiments using EVPmaker and Ethereal, I found it difficult to engage with my imagination in any sustained way. Words or phrases of note appeared infrequently, with no real rhythm or structure. Experimenters say this is normal; the metaphysics of communicating with the dead suggest that the rarity of the voices only demonstrates the process's validity. This argument is at the heart of all EVP phenomena: whether a tape recorder left to record in an empty room or a modified FM radio, the spirit world must work hard to manipulate and transpose whatever bits of electrical noise might float through the ether, and there must be a reason for that work. The energy required by a free-floating consciousness to influence radio frequencies must be enormous, it's said. Therefore, most contemporary forms of EVP are not simply tape recorders in quiet rooms. As Banks makes clear, "most EVP techniques require not the removal, but the addition of extraneous noise to the basic input in order to improve the success and clarity of recordings." The discomforting thing about EVP culture is how literal-minded it is, and except for minor disagreements about where the voices come from, believers and experimenters are in almost complete agreement with Raudive's primary assertion: "The voices are objective entities that can be verified and examined under psycho-acoustic, physical conditions. . . . [T]he voices must therefore be deemed to stem from a different plane of existence than our own." For me, what these researchers miss is that the literalness of their interpretations dissolves any possibility of enchantment. I prefer to think of EVPs as auditory magic lanterns, framed through a secular ritual—that of scientific research—to excite the spiritual imagination.

Like any supernatural phenomenon, EVP is incredibly easy to hoax, and it's almost impossible to set up enough controls to be sure there is no manipulation, even if unintended, on the part of the investigators. Watching YouTube videos of supposed spirit recordings brings this into stark relief. Most EVP videos are subtitled so that what you are hearing is suggested to you, imprinted on your brain, as it were. Trying not to hear what the subtitle suggests the disembodied voice is saying through the radio is challenging. As a test, I closed my eyes while a video played and wrote down what I heard. I then replayed the video and matched what I wrote with the subtitles, and in almost every instance they were different. But then my perception shifted as I took note of the transcribed voice and that became what I heard the second time I watched. In *Breakthrough*, Raudive describes this as being the fault of our hearing. It is very difficult, he writes, to be able to accurately perceive the voices the first time listening. He even suggests that a simple recording only minutes long can take hours to truly understand.

Of course, any recordings of EVPs could be deliberately created to produce the sounds, which is why Donna insists that until you're in a situation where you are doing a recording and hear that first voice, there is no recording that will be absolutely convincing. More important is doing the research, Donna explained, to see if what the voices say has any context. "A lot of researchers fail in their duty," she told me. "They're only interested in voices and not interested in following up on those voices." One sentence, Donna believes, can take you on a journey of discovery. "Who did the voice belong to in life? Is what they said of any value?"

The essential question is, of course, *why* electronic equipment is the method spirits or a disembodied consciousness prefers to communicate through. Donna tried to clarify this for me. It is called "electronic voice phenomena" because, like UFOs (unidentified flying objects), there isn't one blueprint that perfectly frames what is happening. EVP can't be encapsulated in that way, she explained. Some EVPs, like many of those by Jürgenson and Raudive, were recorded with just a microphone and a blank reel of tape, on which the resulting voices are often complete sentences, while the voices captured by a modified radio in the form of what is known as a ghost box (more on these later in Chapter 7) are a series of pockmarked sounds, jumping from syllable to syllable to form single words or names. Donna also sees the human being acting as a conductor of some kind, and sensitive spirit mediums might be particularly powerful antennas helping to draw down the voices between the worlds. Donna calls them human lighthouses, beacons that bring the spirits onto the ports of the physical world. She concedes that sound equipment can also be affected by electromagnetic fields in all kinds of strange ways, picking up everything from baby monitors to Bluetooth radios. She admits, however, that it is futile to try to come up with a grand unified theory of EVP, as there seems to be no continuity to when equipment or techniques will or won't work. "Every time you start building a new theory, it goes out the window because something else happens to completely upset the applecart," she said. Nevertheless, Donna believes that these voices are physical, only occurring within an auditory spectrum we can't hear using our own hearing. Upending the conventional belief held by Raudive that spirits require the electronic equipment to carry their voices into the physical world, Donna suggested that some people can hear the voices without any mediating technologies. EVP mediums have more sensitive ears and a greater range of hearing, sometimes complemented by a hearing aid, such as the Super Ear, a portable device often used by the hard of hearing to amplify sounds of daily life. I knew that my own hearing was likely not powered with superhuman qualities, and in fact years of punk rock shows as a teenager had set me back behind a normal starting line. I was going to have to use technology, and even with electronic devices would have to listen very, very carefully. So, with Donna's encouragement, I started to experiment on my own.

My skepticism has been no ballast against the superstitious tendencies I inherited from my mother, Ruth. Ruth was deeply superstitious in a way that my father steered clear of. He was always the reasonable one, the good-natured stoic who complemented my stubborn, emotional mother. It was a surprise, then, when a few weeks after my mother died, my father called me in a state I can only describe as ecstasy. An unfamiliar bird was happily eating at the feeder in the backyard. My father spotted the bird through the sliding glass door from his reading chair indoors, and was certain it carried within its small downy breast the soul of my mother, his wife—now dead—of forty-two years. Over the phone I could hear the crack in his voice, the desire for belief cutting across his long-treasured rationalism. I knew for him, at that moment, the truth of whether my mother's soul could take flight in a bird was irrelevant to the magic that was conjured in his imagination, igniting and soothing him at once. When the bird chirped, he heard his dead wife's voice announcing she would find a way to be with him in this life. I know my own imagination can produce the same wonders, of seeking serendipity and coincidence, but I was still afraid to try to record EVPs using the Uher reel-to-reel. Because it belonged to my father, and because it was one of the few things I owned that made me feel close to the memory of him, I dreaded hearing his disembodied voice being played back through the machine.

I was deeply interested in using his reel-to-reel to experiment with EVP, but I didn't want to listen back to a recording to hear the voice of my now-late father, even if it was only through some complicated formula of self-suggestion and expectation. Nevertheless, I decided to give it a go. With a reel of new old-stock tape ordered from a dealer online, I set up the machine on my desk, hooked up the microphone, pressed "record," and then followed the advice of Raudive, who in *Breakthrough* suggests politely inviting the spirits to communicate: "Hello, hello . . . I should be very happy to know that the unseen friends are here and are manifesting through the tape."

Whether my father's voice or any other would emerge from my recordings, the process of recording and playing back the tapes took on the quality of a ritual, and like any good sacrament, the suspension of disbelief was potent. Pressing "record," asking questions, and then listening to the playback, I found myself inhabiting states of consciousness not unlike that of looking at Shannon's photographs, of watching *The Tempest* performed at the ART, of working with Nico on my automaton. They each involved a deep concentration and giving over to what may be. It was most like looking at Shannon's photographs after the séance in Lily Dale, however, because I could feel the larger forces of technological history at my back, where I could hear the experimenter's call to investigate, no matter how foolish the endeavor might seem at first. I didn't capture any voices, my father's or otherwise, but while I was experimenting I felt like I was that kid tuning in to his short wave radio hoping to hear the five-note message from outer space, and how that curiosity led me to take apart that very same radio to see if I could put it back together again. Even if one doesn't believe in spirit communication, divination, gods, or magic, using a tape recorder with the intention of capturing spirit voices expands the imagination into realms where ghosts haunt the electromagnetic field, and with the right kind of tinkering, human beings can access the divine, much in the same way the Pepper's Ghost inserts the possibility that the illusion might contain some element of truth. Jeffrey Kripal in his book *The Super Natural* calls this "saying away," where encounters with supernatural or paranormal phenomena allow us to exist in states of reimagining, where we break down preconceptions and then "put things back together in more creative and flourishing ways." This does not require one to become a "believer." It is merely a method to return to a state of enchantment.

Of the EVP culture, it is the DIY spirit that is most intriguing to me. When not used in ways intended, technology exposes the human ability (and desire) to inhabit a mediated place between the imagination and the physical world, in a way that can effect some difference or change. This is especially observable in the DIY maker culture. Both the maker and the magician (aka the spirit medium, the alchemist, or the witch) are in the margins, but more or less as both have to break something that's traditionally thought to be a closed system, something that should be left alone, sanctified. Whether it is a religious prohibition or a cell phone, the magician and the hacker undermine that inviolability. They take things apart, exploring whether it can work in a new way (sometimes at the expense of a warranty, or the threat of their soul). Moreover, they are both agents of their own destiny, be it technological or spiritual. Instead of looking to the spirits for answers, some technology is being used to enhance the person, to alter consciousness in ways that allow us to resonate on these magical frequencies, and to alter our reality to show us where our spiritual destiny might lie.

Ronni Thomas and his Dreamachine, New York, 2017

CHAPTER 6

"In a Light Fantastic Round"

In the office studio of Ronni Thomas, director and producer of the film series The Midnight Archive and self-described Fortean investigator, sat a strange cylindrical object cut with holes of various shapes and sizes placed on top of an old record player. It could very well have been a midcentury modern lamp or a prop from the film *A Clockwork Orange*. Affixed to the ceiling above it was a single light bulb that was positioned halfway down the cylinder. Ronni activated the record player, setting it at 78 rpm, and I watched as the cylinder turned. He then turned on the bulb, and I closed my eyes and leaned in, getting as close to the device as I could without touching it. Flickers of light spun along my eyelids, and for a moment I was not sure I could handle it. But then there was a burst of multicolored shapes, and something inside me let go. I had entered the reality of the Dreamachine.

Sitting together earlier, Ronnie took me back to the moment as a child during a family vacation in Toronto when he realized everyone we know will one day die. He had gotten up from the table at a restaurant to go to the bathroom: "It just rushed into me. Everyone around me is going to die, and everything is going to disappear, and I'm eventually going to die." A journey began, one that would eventually lead him to explore altered states of consciousness, the paranormal, and the occult imagination.

It began in earnest after the day in the restaurant when Ronni began to experience moments of coincidence and intuition that he couldn't easily parse. One such incident was at his Catholic grammar school in Brooklyn, New York, when an infant was found dead and discarded in the school's Dumpster. When the news came out, the school was swarmed by journalists, gawkers, and frantic parents. The mother of the deceased baby lived in the neighborhood near the school, and she spoke to a TV reporter, obviously distraught, asking for help to find the person responsible. Over the next few weeks, the school helped the students process the grim finding, facilitating them in how to manage a tragedy of this kind. During a conversation in the classroom after having seen the distraught mother of the baby on television, Ronni made a bold accusation to the class: "I think she is the one who killed him." He was sent to the principal's office, where he was reproached for being insensitive and rude. Not much later it was reported that, indeed, the mother had killed her child and put the body in the school's Dumpster. Ronni was then pegged as a freak around school, but it only made him more aware of how strange the mind is, and how even stranger the world is. Ronni believed this premonition of sorts was not merely intuition but pointed to some larger mystery about how the mind and world interact.

Ronni began consuming everything he could on paranormal and supernatural phenomena, such as the television show *In Search Of* and then later the *Weekly World News*, the infamous tabloid with headlines like "Hitler's Secret UFO Plans," "Psychic Predicted Time of Own Death," and "Bigfoot Attacks," the intersection of all his interests at the time. It was in the back pages of *Weekly World News* that Ronni discovered the material culture of the supernatural. As an adolescent, he was becoming a consumer of the weird, sending in orders for what was advertised as little paper fortune wheels, books on developing psychic powers, and laminated cards with prayers to various Catholic saints. His mother tried to be patient with all the packages that arrived COD, but it wasn't until the box that contained a voodoo doll that she began to feel some unease at Ronni's all-consuming hobby. This curious little doll—marketed as an occult artifact—would become a springboard for Ronni's own work as a filmmaker. While his interest is in what he calls the immaterial and the ways we have tried to communicate and access it, it's the physical material that provides the fodder for his documentary films: Ouija boards, taxidermy, spirit photography, and automata, to name a few. Ronni explained that our history of supernatural and the occult establishes without a doubt that we have been "trying desperately to communicate" with a higher reality. He likens the physical self to a space suit for our gray matter. It keeps the brain oxygenated and the body mobile, but it prevents us from touching the heavens completely. He is convinced, however, that our consciousness can exist in two places at the same time, materially and in the numinous. Our dreams, a lifelong fascination for Ronni, capture this notion of a shadow world, another reality that involves a special kind of consciousness just as real as our waking state. The lack of any hard evidence in the religious or scientific communities as to what consciousness is has led Ronni to take a DIY approach to his own spiritual development. Like the hacker or maker who builds what is not available or needs the off-the-shelf product to behave in unintended ways, Ronni sees his own consciousness in much the same state. This DIY temperament has served him in a profound way.

Ronni's childhood realization of the reality of death had not personally impacted him until 2010, when a close friend of his died unexpectedly. This was his first personal loss. "Here's somebody who's a little younger than me," he told me, "that just vanished off the face of the Earth." It tossed Ronni out of his orbit, and he was left feeling untethered. A psychiatrist put him on medication. A series of events followed that compounded his anxiety, including family cancer scares. The medication gave him insomnia, so Ambien was prescribed, which Ronni calls "the worst drug." He started to feel unsteady and anxious, and then a friend introduced him to Transcendental Meditation. TM was brought to the United States in 1958 by the Maharishi Mahesh Yogi, who by the 1960s was the face of meditation and Eastern spiritual practice. His tenure as the best-known guru was not without controversy, most notably after the Beatles fled his ashram in India after a spate of accusations that the Maharishi was involved in sexual misdeeds with women. (George Harrison would later regret how things ended with their teacher.) While the popularity of TM waned in popular culture, many continued to practice it as the technique promised freedom from anxiety and worry, as well as deeper spiritual cognition, and has been on an upswing of interest in integrated medical models after multiple empirical studies have shown its effectiveness for a variety of treatments. In 2001, the surrealist filmmaker David Lynch spent a million dollars to participate in a course with the Maharishi himself. A 2013 profile of Lynch by Claire Hoffman for *The New York Times Magazine* says that although Lynch never met the guru personally, the next phase of his life was set. Hoffman writes, "Lynch made his way back to Los Angeles as a changed man." He soon started the David Lynch

Foundation for Consciousness-Based Education and World Peace, which would attract celebrities, writers, and artists from across the spectrum and rekindle an interest in TM worldwide.

After being interviewed by a TM teacher, students are presented with their own personal mantra in the form of a Sanskrit word. Ronni paid the required $1,500 and participated in a four-day course to receive his mantra. While his anxieties and depression weren't completely resolved, practicing TM felt like the first active nontraditional spiritual thing he had participated in, despite his years of studying the occult and arcana. *Now I'm doing*, he thought. *I'm participating.* After some time, his love of life and spirit returned. But he never connected with the mantra he had been given. What if, he thought, he could hack the practice? And then a friend introduced him to a technology called binaural beats.

In 1994, Robert Monroe was granted a patent for "Method of and apparatus for inducing desired states of consciousness," an invention that describes the use of frequency following response (FFR), an effect that can be demonstrated to show that certain types of auditory input can change human brain activity, as measured by Electroencephalography (EEG). The patent shows how FFR can be used to create binaural beats, two digitally crafted tones close in frequency played in each ear via headphones, which produce an illusory third tone, a phenomenon known as "entrainment." Monroe's earlier patent, published in 1975, called "Method of inducing and maintaining various stages of sleep in the human being," showed how certain audio tones could prompt deepening levels of sleep. The 1994 patent, however, demonstrates that entraining can provide more granular levels of not only sleep states but also waking, so as "to enhance the degree of alertness in factory or office workers, as desired." What Monroe never mentions in his patent applications is another purpose he had in mind. Monroe believed his inventions could induce out-of-body experiences (OBE) and other spiritual states of consciousness. The related trademark for his patent, Hemi-Sync, is a bit more candid: "Research in the field of self-discovery and consciousness exploration." The Hemi-Sync technology now plays a vital role in courses on self-development and consciousness exploration offered by his organization, the Monroe Institute, founded in 1985.

Monroe first discovered the possibilities of entrainment in 1956, when he began experimenting with the relationship between sound and sleep states. He sought answers to questions such as: Could we listen to tapes at certain frequencies while sleeping and learn a foreign language? The results of his tests were like nothing he had imagined. During one research session, Monroe experienced his first out-of-body experience, which he describes in his book *Journeys Out of the Body* as "a sledge-hammer blow" to his rational scientific worldview, and one that he writes, "Shattered my faith in the totality and certainty of our culture's scientific knowledge." Over the course of a few nights, Monroe had a series of uncomfortable and sometimes frightening sensations while lying in bed. They began with a painful stomachache, which resolved itself in a sense of a high-frequency vibration coursing through his body. One night it felt as though he could put his hand through the floor and touch a water source underground. The greatest shock came, however, when he saw himself in bed next to his wife and thought he was dying. He had little control over what was happening, until one evening he exerted as much will as he could and was able to rise and "smoothly floated up over the bed." He dubbed the condition of being outside one's body as "Second State" or "Second Body," deliberately avoiding using "astral projection" for the term's occult associations. He then began a life's work of investigating the phenomenon he had experienced, and most important, how one might deliberately provoke it to happen.

The overall tone of *Journeys Out of the Body* is clearheaded and rational, objectively documenting the stories of those who claim to have "left" their bodies. Monroe's own OBE story, however, is recounted as a series of bizarre incidents for which he gives no explanation. He credits the origin of his OBEs as a "beam or ray [that] seemed to come out of the sky to the north at about a 30° angle from the horizon." Monroe writes that beam struck him and caused him to "shake violently or 'vibrate.'" I sent an e-mail to the Monroe Institute asking about the ray, and for clarification as to what they thought the source of the beam might have been. Carol Munroe (no relation), the program assistant, immediately wrote me back to say that no one at the institute knew the answer. During his life, she told me, Robert Monroe had speculated—based on a friend's suggestion— that the "pyramid shaped roof of his house might have facilitated the experience," which he recounts in his second book, *Far Journeys*, published in 1985, calling to mind the once-popular new age fad known as pyramid power, which he may have been influenced by after the actual OBEs.

Pyramid power originates in a legendary account by Antoine Bovis, a French hardware store owner and amateur dowser who coined the term. While there is no evidence Bovis ever went to Egypt, the apocryphal origin story has him visiting the Great Pyramid of Cheops in Egypt. This particular pyramid has a long history of curious speculation regarding its purpose and ancestry after hidden chambers were discovered by archaeologists, information Bovis would have been aware of. During his tour, it is said he noticed that stray animals had sometimes found their way into the pyramid only to become lost and eventually die. When discovered along the tour path, guides would toss the bodies into a trash bin found in the King's Chamber. But Bovis claims he never smelled decomposition and further saw that the animals showed no signs of decay, only desiccation. He went home to expound on the notions and belief that unique properties of pyramidal shapes could act as a giant dowsing pendulum, slowing down the process of putrefaction. Bovis embarked on his own experiments to test this by building a small pyramid out of wood and placing deceased animals in the structure. None decayed, or so Bovis wrote in a self-published pamphlet detailing the study and its results. There, he concludes that the King's Chamber of the Great Pyramid of Cheops was also a lab where similar experiments were performed.

Pyramid power first entered popular consciousness in 1970s through Patrick Flanagan's 1973 book *Pyramid Power*. In it, he cites Bovis's discovery as the event that led to the discovery of the pyramid's potential. In *Pyramid Power*, Flanagan traces the idea of spiritual energy that is described by many religious traditions, including the Hindu *prana* (breath), Chinese *chi*, and the life force—discovered in 1845 by Carl von Reichenbach via what he called *od*, all essentially different names for the same energy, which, according to Flanagan, can be collected and manipulated by use of a pyramidal structure. Flanagan takes it further by claiming that pyramids can increase alpha wave functions in a human body when small versions are placed over the head of someone meditating or otherwise seeking altered states of consciousness. Supporting his claim, his test subjects reported "intense heat in the body and tingling sensations in the hand," a noteworthy reverberation of Monroe's description of his first OBEs.

Which brings us back to Monroe and his speculation that the pyramid-shaped roof of his house impelled his OBEs. It's arguably not a far stretch to connect Flanagan's and Bovis's descriptions of vibrations in the body with Monroe's later testimony that he had been hit with an energy ray, incidents that call up images of extraterrestrial intervention. Indeed, OBEs and a belief in alien intelligences are often paired. One of Monroe's students, Rosalind A. McKnight, published *Cosmic Journeys: My Out-Of-Body Explorations with Robert A. Monroe* in 1999. McKnight explicitly details her own engagement with aliens during an OBE session directed by Monroe himself. In her account, during her time away from terrestrial conscious inhabitation, aliens communicate with her that they are "guardians of the Earth" and impart the message that "we must clean up both our polluted minds and planet." In another encounter, she depicts the aliens placing a pyramid over her, filling her with energy. She is then guided to a larger pyramid and directed to walk to the top, where again she is permeated with energy and vibrations. Something even more astounding happens to her. McKnight describes having another, second OBE within the current one, like a dream within a dream, seeing her "self" out of her body, on the pyramid. This lends cosmic significance to Monroe's first experience by suggesting that the energy beam Monroe claims penetrated him, and which may have been given amplitude by his pyramid-shaped roof, was extraterrestrial in origin. In *Far Journeys*, Monroe described interactions with otherworldly intelligences by a team of people—dubbed the Explorers—who became incredibly proficient using the Hemi-Sync technology in achieving OBEs. During a series of experiments, the Explorers continued to meet "intelligent beings who were more or less willing to communicate—and could do so," often by speaking through the Explorers, possibly using advanced technology. The Explorers were taught that there are twenty-eight levels of consciousness, and that the energy of human beings is siphoned by higher levels, planted in a cosmic garden, harvested as a substance called "loosh," and then consumed by the entities.

Monroe found that his binaural tones, which could produce FFRs, were the most effective means of helping people achieve OBEs, but only after they have incorporated the idea that "consciousness is a form of energy at work" and have learned how to perceive it. Using Hemi-Sync technology, Monroe says, is more of an assist to a state of being that requires practice. Experimenters are urged to use an affirmation that begins, "I am more than my physical body. Because I am more than physical matter, I can perceive that which is greater than the physical world." Monroe makes clear in *Journeys Out of the Body* that not everyone can have an out-of-body experience. But for those who can, Monroe teaches, an OBE is the most effective means of attesting to the dream that our consciousness survives death. With decades of experience under his belt, Monroe published *Ultimate Journey* in 1994, writing that not only are sound-directed OBEs proof that "survival of self beyond physical existence is a natural and automatic process," but that OBE states can enable people to contact loved ones who have died. Monroe cautions that this must be done soon after the person has passed away, as these untethered consciousnesses "rapidly lose interest in the life they have just completed."

The Monroe Institute thrives, offering classes and retreats that use some version of sound technology to enable "human consciousness exploration," providing programs on lucid dreaming, near-death experiences intended to free one from fear of dying, and even remote viewing (the ability to see things over vast distances using a kind of inner sight). Almost all the work done at the institute involves Monroe's inventions, which lends a scientific foundation to the work of transcendence. Wavering around the edges at a barely discernible frequency is the strange origin story of Monroe's methods and the source of the knowledge: a complex spiritual cosmology made up of varying degrees of consciousness, beings of pure energy who eat our life force, advanced alien science, and the revelation that we live on after our bodies die.

At the top of this citadel of occult resonances sits Monroe's patented sound technology, an important public measure and confirmation that the United States government, no less, agrees that what he has designed works. Of course, the patents themselves are merely for the mechanism to create binaural tones, not for their efficacy in aiding travel beyond the body. The current we have been riding from the earliest uses of technology to create supernatural resonances is the same: technology is rational, and moreover, crafted by human hands, which demonstrates—to those who believe—that we can complete the circuit needed to connect us to the divine.

In an insightful moment of spiritual hacking, instead of using the mantra, Ronni meditated while listening to the beats. Inserting technology into his TM practice was a radical and transformative moment. Like any good hack it was both disruptive and practical. Moreover, it revealed that spiritual exercises were not in conflict with the material world. Like many of the examples we have investigated thus far, the use of technology is the bridge over that vast channel separating the phenomenal from the numinous. Here, technology is not the tool that allows the spirit world—or that part of our imaginations—to cross over, but redirects our brains to achieve states of consciousness that enliven our imaginations. "It truly was just the sound that I was looking for," Ronni told me.

Ronni would go even further in his experiments after his thirty-eighth birthday, when his wife gave him a Dreamachine she had built herself. It proved itself to be the missing component. As a filmmaker, he always felt TM to be wanting because he couldn't find a way to connect to the visual aspect of the internal experience. When he first tried it, Ronni found it lacking, nothing like that described by the musician Andrew McKenzie, who wrote that the Dreamachine "facilitates access to finer and rarer rates of vibrations and planes of existence." Ronni found it interesting, but couldn't communicate with that higher consciousness he had been in search of. He tried not to anticipate seeing anything or achieving an altered state, remembering the most important lesson of his TM training: "Have no expectation." But here, Ronni was swapping sound (originally in the form of a mantra and then the binaural beats) for a visually induced state. It was the combination of the two that determined a powerful spiritual tool. By adding the binaural beats to his device, he found that elusive piece of the puzzle, allowing for an experience of transcendence he never found with TM. The Dreamachine produces states that are unique among these kinds of technologies. Its inventor, Brion Gysin (1916–1986)—the late surrealist writer and artist—once described the Dreamachine as having culture-altering potential and "may bring about a change in consciousness inasmuch as it throws back the limits of the visible world and may, indeed, prove that there are no limits." Gysin was so convinced of the machine's potential that he believed a conspiracy was afoot to prevent people from achieving the altered states of consciousness it offers, to ensure the status quo of capitalist consumer culture. Criminalizing hallucinogenic and other drugs was the method the government used. Gysin believed the conspiracy included corporations and the media, as evidenced by his inability to find a company to mass-produce his wondrous flicker device or media outlet that would share the news. The Dreamachine, he said, may make it "possible to become something more than a man."

The invention of the Dreamachine was completely by chance. On a bus trip to an artist's retreat near Marseilles, France, in 1958, Gysin was gazing out the window at a tree-lined street when the dappled reflection of the sun streaming through the branches required him to close his eyes. As soon as he did so, he was overcome by a "transcendental storm": a barrage of kaleidoscopic patterns and colors in the inside of his eyelids that created a feeling he describes as being "swept out of time." Gysin later learned the phenomenon is called flicker, first described by W. Grey Walter in his 1953 book *The Living Brain*. Grey describes performing experiments on test subjects "by the flickering of a powerlight in the eyes," and the resulting EEG readings showed increased alpha wave activity. The test subjects reported seeing "whirling spirals, whirlpools, explosions, Catherine wheels." Pulsing at a certain frequency, flicker can bring people into the next level, known as theta.

The theta state, often characterized as the moment just before you fall asleep, is also called hypnagogia. People often report visual or auditory hallucinations and visions, such as hearing a loud noise or clap that immediately pulls you out of the state. (I sometimes hear a voice loudly saying, "Hello," and I sense it directly in my ear.) The surrealist Salvador Dalí offered instructions for how to achieve this state, which he called "slumber with a key." He recommended sitting upright in a chair, ceramic plate on the floor between your feet, and holding a key very lightly "pressed between the extremities of the thumb and forefinger of your left hand" so that just as you fall asleep you drop the key and are startled awake when the clatter of metal hitting ceramic is heard. That very short but liminal place is the theta state and where Dalí believed potent creative thoughts could be accessed. Using the Dreamachine, it is believed, can keep you in this state for an extended period, but there is reason to accept the idea that it works on our psyches much in the same way magical performance and ritual do. In an online research paper, "The Clinical Guide to Sound and Light," the author Thomas Budzynski notes that Aristotle believed the hypnagogic state could be encouraged by a certain kind of poetic rhetoric called "psychagogia," or "soul leading." The performance of mythic tragedy in particular can alter the state of the spectator as it can transport the spectator to a state between their conscious and unconscious mind.

Gysin needed someone to build a small-scale device capable of producing the flicker effect and conscripted Ian Sommerville, a young computer and electronics whiz who was part of the social network of Gysin's collaborators and friends, as well as having once been the lover of writer William Burroughs. Sommerville's device could be cheaply reproduced and didn't require any special laboratory or other equipment to make use of it. *Dream Machine*, a retrospective look at Gysin's work, calls the machine that Sommerville made "one of the most important innovations of Gysin's artistic career," as it represented a kind of telescopic view of the most primal archetypes of the human psyche.

In the early 1960s, plans for a homemade Dreamachine began to circulate, but it wasn't until Gysin met the musician and performance artist Genesis Breyer P-Orridge that a wider swath of the counterculture took interest in the device. P-Orridge—one of the founding members of the notorious performance art collective COUM, the industrial rock outfit Throbbing Gristle, and the visionary leader of the band Psychic TV—believed that media was a form of cultural control, and could be reimagined as a magical weapon against the autocracy. William Burroughs had introduced P-Orridge to Gysin, and P-Orridge would become Gysin's most important spiritual benefactor, introducing his art divination method known as "cut ups" to a much wider network of artists and art consumers. P-Orridge believed the most powerful means of challenging the system was through the expansion of consciousness, be it through magic or art. Either way, the Dreamachine offered a direct and potent means to get there.

––––––

A few years before Ronni was experimenting with his Dreamachine, volume 10 of the magazine *Make:* published in 2007 presented a project that could be built with basic electronic components and a microcontroller. Called "The Brain Machine," the article by Mitch Altman opens with the subheading, "You don't have to be a Buddhist monk to meditate." By flashing LEDs onto your closed eyes and sending binaural beats into your ears, the final product's effects can supposedly alter brain wave frequencies to create different states of consciousness. This brain machine slowly guides the brain from its normal beta wave state to a deep meditative state by pulsing the light at varying frequencies matched in rate by the binaural beats. A *Make:* reader and seeker myself, I, of course, undertook the project and, following the instructions, built the device. Small LEDs are inserted into the lenses of a pair of safety glasses, and a headphone jack, a small battery pack, and a few other components are wired to the microcontroller. A bit of code is uploaded, and then once they were complete, I placed them over my eyes, plugged in the headphones, and turned them on. The intensity of the light pulses was challenging and off-putting, but I took a few deep breaths and let go, allowing the lights and sounds to lead me into the deeper realms of my mind.

Mitch Altman is a San Francisco–based hacker and inventor who was well known in the DIY community for inventing the TV-B-Gone remote control, a small key chain that can turn off TVs in public places. In the 1980s, he did pioneering work in virtual reality, then cofounded a successful Silicon Valley start-up in the late 1990s, and has since been lecturing and teaching how to solder and make things using microcontrollers. I spoke with Mitch about his brain machine project in *Make:*, and he explained that what led him to create the device was to offer a cheaper, hackable DIY version of comparable devices that are available commercially and sell for hundreds of dollars. Building his own Dreamachine wouldn't suffice, given what he sees as its limitations. Since the Dreamachine creates a single continual alpha wave frequency, he explained, the user can't go into deeper states of consciousness. Ronni Thomas dealt with this by adding binaural beats into the experience. By using a microcontroller, Mitch can program his brain machine to produce a specific meditation sequence, using many different frequencies to create deeper states. It can then stay at a set of brain wave frequencies for a period and, without using an external timer, bring the user back to a waking state.

Mitch has been meditating since he was thirteen years old, during a time when he was profoundly depressed. The practice became the centerpiece of a life of self-discovery: "I've done work on myself, learned to live a life I really love living. And it was a long road, but meditation was a big, important part of all of that." Mitch wanted others to benefit with the same positive outcomes he had with meditation. Being a tinkerer, a hacker, and an entrepreneur, he turned to technology. The Dreamachine as a concept was easily reimagined as something portable and programmable.

Mitch helped me understand and recognize the hacker as an agent of spiritual change and rebellion. He described hacking as a state of being, a way of looking at the material and natural world that provides a variety of resources such as fossil fuels, minerals, and metals, as well as those constructed by humans to serve humanity, such as paper, money, or developable skills and intelligences. As Mitch explained, the hacker makes use of all these resources to advance their projects, whether it's making a device useful to the individual, of service to the community, or in the case of the brain machine, living their life to the best of their ability—and beyond. Whatever the project, hackers make use of these resources any way they want, and "not just the way that those resources were intended to be used." The hacker often disseminates and shares, in the spirit of the open-source philosophy, to make their work freely available and, in the language of the open-source license known as Creative Commons, "to share, repurpose, and remix." This dissemination often happens on the edges of the mainstream, in online forums and electronic repositories, and at hacker and maker gatherings.

Not unlike the hacker creed, magical and occult practices also rely on natural and human resources, often remixed and repurposed in ways not originally intended. It thwarts what is prescribed, customary, or expected, toward further as-yet-unimagined possibilities for people and things. As described earlier, this once involved using the corresponding forces of stones and plants that were believed to be able to activate certain divine and planetary forces. Taking the hacker mentality further, the universe can be resource manipulated to affect change, often in service to the practitioner's or magician's will. Most important, the human being is the agent of this change, inserting themselves into the natural course of things to reimagine reality and to direct their will toward a certain outcome. Mitch's brain machine perfectly encapsulates this interchange between hacker and occultist, applying human agency to technology to break open the spiritual imagination. "Hacking really is magic," Mitch told me. "You're starting with an idea that does not exist as anything except a thought or feeling, and then over some period of time you manifest that idea into reality."

The brain machine registers across both the DIY and hacker

sensibilities in interesting ways, most obviously because it is built and can be modified by the user. At the same time, it presents an opportunity for a more direct relationship with the techniques that can induce altered states of consciousness. Traditional methods such as meditation, ecstatic dancing, and ritual can also be self-directed activities, but typically don't involve the same inventive spirit we have been following. Such states are also available via hallucinogenic drugs, methods shown to create experiences similar in kind if not degree to classical mystical ones. These parallels were first noted by William James in his 1902 *Varieties of Religious Experience*, where four categories or features of most mystical experiences are described: ineffability (beyond words), noetic (deep and divine truths are revealed), transiency (the experience is fleeting), and passivity (mystical states happen to us without will). In recorded history to date, almost all religious cultures and practices have required extended periods of training or preparation, as well as initiatory rites mediated by those deemed with authority to guide others to either piety or higher states of consciousness. Certainly, there is still an appreciation for observing traditions, practiced as close to their origins as we know of. Nevertheless, as humans and society change over time, it's interesting to note that this hacker subculture of a new generation, one born in the rapidly changing technological world of a nation that values independence and entrepreneurial spirit, would come out of the United States.

Even after a few tries of the brain machine, I could recognize its potential as a method for hacking traditional meditation disciplines, in much the same way Ronni uses technology to rejigger his TM practice. Alone, the Dreamachine offers visuals that are akin to a hallucinogenic state, but the mind is still actively in control. The binaural beats offer a kind of electronic mantra that enables true transcendental potential.

The brain machine works on many of the same principles, but Mitch's innovation was to use the light and the beat to *direct* the user through the meditative experience. With the Dreamachine I felt a little unmoored, unsure of how I was supposed to feel or how deep I was supposed to go, unguided and perhaps out of control. The brain machine, on the other hand, guided me through the states as if with a mentor, teacher, or guru. At one point, it felt like I was rushing down a tunnel toward a bright, luminescent figure, not unlike what one of Robert Monroe's Explorers describes in *Far Journeys* as "a transparent, radiating tube." Moving rapidly down a tunnel or tube is a common feature of OBE descriptions. One of the remarkable qualities of the brain machine is that the flickering LEDs and the binaural beats are integrated such that it produces a synesthesia-like effect. It is impossible to separate the pulsing beat from the visual effect of a tunnel, as though the beats were the engine propelling me forward. Unexpected questions arose. Was this all an illusion of the device? A standard response of the biological brain? Maybe a previously unexperienced state of consciousness was being opened. Maybe my mind was simply having a response to what my brain was perceiving. Maybe Monroe was right, and I was being led toward some greater spiritual reality. I never did break into anything I would call an OBE, but further use of the brain machine offered varying and different degrees of these sensations. One also wonders what my experience would have been like had I not already been steeped in the background and intention of these methods and devices. It was tempting to think of this as not only an aid, but perhaps a substitute, for a meditation practice.

This begs the question: Should we use technology to quicken the pace toward spiritual states of being? This question was at the core of early thinking about altered states of consciousness and their origin as religious experiences. In 1939, the author Aldous Huxley had begun his own spiritual journey as a student of the Hindu religious philosophy known as Vedanta. Vedanta—the philosophical underpinning of Hinduism—teaches that *brahman*, the unified Godhead, and *atman*, the human soul, are not distinct manifestations but are a unified divine continuum. Yoga, a spiritual discipline involving asanas (or poses), fasting, and meditation, can sweep away the illusion that we are separate from God. Huxley hoped a recognition of our divine nature could help heal a Western material and spiritual crisis. But this meant work, a commitment to spiritual ideals, and lots of meditation. Either that, or four-tenths of a gram of mescaline.

Administered by his friend the psychiatrist Humphry Osmond, Huxley's mescaline trip revealed to him a holy-infused world that is essentially filtered out by our brains so as to not overwhelm us. Huxley contended that brains have developed a kind of evolutionary protection to ensure survival by mediating the flood of reality, predicting our perceptions based on previous experience, sorting through sensory input, selecting what we remember, and tossing the rest. Years of disciplined spiritual practice have the potential to open the valve or separate function from perception, or a drug like mescaline releases the floodgates to show us our true nature in context of the cosmos. Huxley's experience is detailed in his essential *Doors of Perception*, published in 1954, where he writes, "The Beatific Vision, Sat Chit Ananda, Being-Awareness-Bliss for the first time I understood, not on the verbal level, not by inchoate hints or at a distance, but precisely and completely what those prodigious syllables referred to." After his mescaline experience, Huxley was no longer convinced that visionary states of consciousness were the purview of the spiritually gifted. Huxley saw his previous beliefs as a kind of folly. What he knew was true about fasting and meditation could also be achieved by a few micrograms of mescaline. Further, that traditional visionary and hallucinogenic states are not only equivalent, but the latter is the better option. To spend a lifetime meditating in the hopes of achieving enlightenment when mescaline can deliver it to you in an instant is as ludicrous as, Huxley writes, the man who "burned down the house in order to roast the pig." While this view is one that has been debated for decades, the introduction of a different kind of mechanism for breaking through to altered states has only raised more questions about what those states really are.

Mitch agreed that you can get to the same states much more quickly if you take a drug like LSD, mescaline, or psilocybin (the active compound found in hallucinogenic mushrooms) or with a device like the brain machine, which uses sensory inputs to guide you there. In fact, Mitch told me, the original name of the project was "guide glasses." Regular use of the glasses can help you get to these altered states faster than a consistent meditation practice, but their inventor admits that when you use these shortcuts, you don't get the benefit of a lifetime of practice. The brain machine offers something of a middle way, presenting an opportunity to have glimpses of these states as well as learn from them. The state is beneficial for a time, but the goal of meditation and other spiritual practices, Mitch believes, is something a bit more of the mundane. Quoting an ancient Chinese saying, Mitch suggests, "When the common person becomes enlightened, they become a sage, and when a sage becomes enlightened they become a common person." A lifetime of practice is what it takes to become better at living your life, Mitch believes. "It's not about being in a particular state. It's about living a life that you find worthwhile."

Huston Smith, a great scholar of world religion, once presented a similar line of thought. Smith was one of the early proponents of psychedelic drugs and their usefulness for achieving religious states of consciousness. He first took psilocybin during the infamous Harvard Psilocybin Project, a research study led by Timothy Leary and Ram Dass (then Richard Alpert) from 1960 to 1962 at Harvard University, but soon became disenchanted with psychedelic culture, worried that people had created a religion that was nothing more than a series of visionary experiences, with no content or guidance on how to live and be in the day to day. The drugs didn't guarantee leading users to an ethical, purposeful life beyond just continually having those experiences repeatedly, making no contribution to the community at large. Mitch had similar thoughts during the time he spent in India, where he spent time in a large ashram composed of many Westerners who appeared to him to be lost. The ashram was not a springboard toward a better life at home. It was a churning eddy in a swift, deep river. Mitch believes that learning under a guru, taking a drug, or using the Dreamachine are beneficial experiences, but rejects anything that offers a perpetual "warm and fuzzy" spiritual stagnation. Mitch prefers the role of a caretaker and facilitator, making these experiences available to others who can benefit from them, "and then go off into their life."

Similarly, as Huston Smith warns, visionary and altered states of consciousness can become addicting. As a teenager, Mitch himself had once used LSD as a way of avoiding taking responsibility for living his life. Drugs, Mitch thinks, can give a person already disconnected from life in their community or on the planet a window into how bizarre and unfathomable the universe really is, and that there are possibilities such that one might not have imagined. "But after a while, you don't need the drugs anymore. You learned what you can from the drugs, and just from having this altered perception of things, then you can start all of what I think of as the real work, which is even more fascinating." Similarly, Mitch told me, devices like the brain machine that can expand consciousness become a guidepost training for you to be able to access a heightened state using more traditional methods, like meditation. After a while, Mitch revealed, you don't need the device anymore at all.

The brain machine poses a problem on the periphery of the use of technology to engage with occult and supernatural realities, in whatever form they might take. We have seen that devices, whether in the form of a camera used to photograph ectoplasm, an automaton that registers along the uncanny spectrum, an EVP recording, or even a ritual performance that uses robots, aid our ability to alter our recognition and understanding of reality and our place in it, but perhaps these tools only offer a glimpse of the varying states of being that ultimately demand another kind of engagement. The EVP recording of Raudive, for example, created a loop of meaning much like that which Huston Smith points out, never moving beyond self-referencing. The supposed truth that our souls live on after death revealed by EVPs doesn't present any other modes of action, nor does it create a set of values that can uplift our day-to-day lives. I am playing my own devil's advocate here to make the point Mitch wants us to learn from his brain machine: at some point, we must let go of technology to really get to our full human potential. The technology is the vehicle but not the destination.

This tension plays out in dramatic ways in the debates around transhumanism, a movement designed to elevate, enhance, and ultimately transform human beings via technology. This final merging of the human and the machine is called the singularity, a term coined by futurist and entrepreneur Ray Kurzweil. The singularity will occur when human beings have transferred their consciousness into computers, a state of immortality Kurzweil calls "spiritual machines." While most transhumanists are concerned with the betterment and potential immortality of the human being, there has always been a subtle religious and spiritual subtext to the movement often called posthumanism. The more conservative transhumanist posits that with technology, we will be able to extend our mental capacity, our physical limitations, and our lives, possibly leading to immortality. In this respect, God and religion are irrelevant; simply superstitious ideas keep us from moving science in the direction leading to the discoveries and inventions that will shape our imaginable destiny. Posthumanists see themselves as the next step beyond transhumanism, where even the body is no longer a boundary. They see the human being as a web of data that can be uploaded into other vessels, and will one day even transcend the limitations of terrestrial Earth. To this end, humanity will achieve a kind of godhood; indeed, some posthumanists believe our own species was created by "gods" from another, much older civilization that have become truly posthuman. For some transhumanists, this kind of spiritual-inflected language is a distraction, but for many posthumanists, humans must come to terms with the spiritual and religious aspects of our humanity. In either case, spiritual ideas must be reckoned with.

At the core of all transhumanist philosophy lie these spiritual inquiries. As the writer Meghan O'Gieblyn notes in her illuminating article for *N+1* (excerpted in the *Guardian*), transhumanism reinserts a religious aspiration into a rational materialist vision, as it "promises to restore, through science, the transcendent hopes that science itself has obliterated." The notion of soul is replaced by the idea of mind, but what remains is a dualistic notion of the body as somehow distinct from *self.*

Descartes's automaton clicks into motion again with the transhumanist vision of a "ghost in the machine," where the container is partly irrelevant to the spirit that winds it up and keeps it going. As we also saw, the nineteenth-century Spiritualists thought along similar lines. In the 1889 book *The Religion of Spiritualism*, the author Samuel Watson describes the spirit as the engine of the body: "Spirit acts upon matter, controls it, imparts the life it possesses, gives it will, organization, being." Transhumanists, calling spirit "mind," believe we will one day determine "how to liberate the mind from its dying carrier, the brain inside the body." What sets transhumanists apart from the supernatural and religious categories of thought is that technology is the means through which this ascension into immortality will occur. Even so, some EVP enthusiasts believe that the voices they receive could very well be our future transhuman selves attempting to make contact.

The body, for the transhumanist, is a strangely imperfect vessel, not only mortal, but subject to breakage and illness, and limited in its capacity to survive beyond the most precise conditions of air, water, and temperature. Uploading the mind, whether into a computer or a robotic assembly, could allow for not only immortality, but opportunities for explorations into space never before thought possible. The futurist and roboticist Hans Moravec calls the process of uploading "transfiguration" a clear nod to the Christian story that, after his death, Jesus becomes an immortal divine being. Moreover, it also squares nicely with the Christian idea of the bodily resurrection, where during the rapture, the bodies of the dead will rise anew and be perfected. Transhumanism also contains the seeds of how technology and the supernatural have always functioned together where the human being takes hold of their spiritual fate through innovation and invention. O'Gieblyn writes that her own encounter with transhumanism offered "an evolutionary approach to eschatology, one in which humanity took it upon itself to bring about the final glorification of the body."

It's no surprise, then, that one of the most vocal religious proponents of transhumanism is the Mormon Transhumanist Association, whose logo is a wooden wheel with a set of angel wings emerging from each side, a symbol capturing both the inventive and religious spirit. As described in Chapter 5, Mormonism was founded on the belief that Joseph Smith used a type of magical technology to discover and read the tablets that would form the basis of his new religion. During the 2014 conference Religion and Transhumanism in Piedmont, California, the Mormon speaker was Lincoln Cannon—a self-described "technologist and philosopher" and founder of the Mormon Transhumanist Association—who illuminated how Mormonism and transhumanism are deeply compatible. First, Cannon notes that Mormons believe miracles are not supernatural, but rather obey natural laws we have not yet discovered. Like the medieval definition of natural magic, miracles reveal yet-uncovered workings of the universe. Second, Mormons see themselves not as followers of Christian creed, but "an aspiration to live the religion of Jesus," and to become "gods and saviors." Cannon calls prophecy interactive. In a profound deepening of the Protestant idea of being responsible for one's own salvation, Mormons believe prophecies are not determined but show what might be, and the human being can change the outcome. The use of technology to effect this change is merely one tool that a Mormon can use. In 1844, Joseph Smith, preaching to an assembly of Mormons, urged them "to learn how to be gods yourselves," and transhumanist Mormons accept this challenge and the technological means through which this might occur. Cannon goes on to say that the idea of the singularity syncs up with the Christian doctrine of the return to Christ to presage in a new Golden Age. The Celestial City, Mormons believe, is not in heaven but on Earth, and transhumanist Mormons imagine it could take the form not unlike what a futurist might envision and that Kurzweil himself thinks possible: a world free of disease and death, where the human mind (or soul) inhabits perfect robotic bodies, and where we are able to travel the cosmos as bits of information, pinging from galaxy to galaxy like angels. Christ himself, Cannon notes, might even return as a form of artificial intelligence showing us the way. While Cannon and other Mormon transhumanists would likely disagree, these beliefs point back to Mormonism's own history using forms of magic—particularly in its proto-technological forms such as dowsing rods and seeing stones—as the future salvation of the world depends not only on human intervention, but will rely on our capacity to reimagine the uses of technology in ways usually thought to be antithetical to their intended purpose.

The most critical take on transhumanism stems from these undeniable supernatural features that seem to be inherent in the movement, despite it often pushing hard against any notion of supernaturalism. In an article for *The New Atlantis* titled "Why Transhumanism Won't Work," physicist Mark Gubrud pulls apart the idea of uploading the human mind into a computer or robot by noting that "arguments for identity transfer cannot be stated without invoking nonphysical entities." Science has not discovered whether consciousness is somehow distinct from the brain, and Gubrud maintains that any suggestion that mind or self exists as a thing in itself is calling on the supernatural notion of a soul. He even likens uploading our consciousness to what is known as sympathetic magic, whereby "a voodoo priest can capture a soul and imprison it in a doll." He concludes with no compromise: "Uploading cannot work . . . as a way for people to escape death and transcend to existence as a technological super-being."

Mitch is also skeptical about transhumanism and worries that the movement is about trying to avoid the pain of exploring oneself. Mitch likens the addictive potential of technological power to that of money and financial power. Every person Mitch has talked to that considers themselves transhumanist wants to one day upload their consciousness to a computer so they can live forever, or they are focused on various means of life extension so they can live longer. Mitch doesn't have qualms with the person who loses an arm and uses technology to create a prosthetic limb, because in that case, they're trying to hack their body to enable them to simply be more normally human rather than more powerfully human. But the line for Mitch is blurry. While he is a proponent of hacking and finding innovative ways to use traditional tools, he doesn't want technology to lift him out of the conditions of his own life. His brain machine is not meant to be a form of escapism but a method for going deeper inside oneself.

Ronni amplified his ideas about how Gysin's Dreamachine can function, and his description looks a lot like magic. Ronni believes that other than the things necessary for our human bodies, our brain has a more invisible purpose, which is to receive transmitted consciousness from some external intelligence. Living in the material world and centuries of positivist thinking have, Ronni said, "detuned our frequencies," and it has become harder to communicate with that external intelligence. We once had a much more "direct line" to whatever it is that is the source of consciousness, but over time those senses have dulled. For Ronni, the Dreamachine is the purest version of that experience. Not only has it deepened Ronni's spiritual path, but he sees the practical benefits as well. Ronni believes using the Dreamachine has made him a better filmmaker, producing material he is much more pleased with.

Ronni also likened the Dreamachine as corresponding to states of mind that allowed him to, as a child, deduce that the mother had been the killer of her own child. It's not merely intuition, Ronni clarified, but rather demonstration of transcendence, of how our consciousness can interact with a higher order of reality, where other kinds of knowledge might be available. This is not so far removed from what Monroe would teach, and Ronni also believes that we're all capable of achieving these states. But it does take an active pursuit. Ronni calls it binary communication, and lends another level of technological language to ancient practices such as divination and spirit contact. It is, of course, more than simply our imaginations at work. To talk about transcendence in this way means we are talking about something that's beyond our perceptual reality, and this is what Ronni thinks we are coming around to more and more. The increased interest in EVPs, the glut of television programs and films about ghost hunting, supernatural found footage, and haunted technologies (at the time of this writing, a new film was in the works titled *Polaroid*, about a vintage Polaroid camera that predicts the violent death of whoever's photo is taken), as well as an overall increased interest in occultism and magic, demonstrate how starved we are for expressions of transcendence, even if only in our pop culture. Often, occult beliefs gain popular traction during times of great cultural upheaval. As noted, the occult and related alternative religious practices give people a sense of having agency over their own spiritual and inner lives. Just as conspiracy theories help people feel like there is order in the chaos of world events, occultism and belief in the supernatural offer a similar balm. Moreover, the occult gives people and artists—such as the photographer Shannon Taggart—a means to challenge the mainstream, to push up against convention, even if only to play with those images and ideas. Second, the occult gives people a means to exert power and control over their own spiritual (and cultural) destinies. It's a place where folks can feel like they can do something that matters. And certainly, both come out of a time when people are feeling helpless politically or are eager for change.

But Ronni suggested whatever truth might be revealed may not come from an EVP, a Ouija board, or a spirit rapping on a table. There is, Ronni believes, a force we don't quite understand, and may discover within a new kind of quantum mechanics. The Dreamachine inhabits a space that allows these realities to transpose themselves into our imaginations, much like hallucinogenic drugs, but even more so like a shamanic practice that uses sights and sounds to create altered states for their worshippers. The Dreamachine doesn't have the same dramatic effect as those, but it mirrors the realities those practices make manifest. As Ronni told me, "A machine with a spinning light bulb and binaural beats [is] a technological version of chants, a fire, and somebody dancing." We know that many shamanic performances were once aided by hallucinogenic drugs, and Huxley, writing in *Heaven and Hell*, his follow-up to *Doors of Perception*, imagined that using stroboscopic light along with drugs might speed up the visionary experience to an enormous degree.

Sitting up with my face barely an inch from the Dreamachine, the beats generating unfamiliar frequencies in my ears, I began to feel a little afraid. An idea or a feeling I wasn't quite sure I wanted to capture was waiting for me in the stroboscopic display of shapes and colors passing along my closed eyelids. I have had my own experiences with altered states of consciousness in the past, and I was reminded of those moments here, particularly in the feeling that just around the corner is some great truth waiting for me. I knew I could pull my face away whenever I wanted to, but I felt glued to the machine, even as I was unsure if I would be able to withstand the encounter. My skepticism was also playing a role here, second-guessing every whirl and pattern as mere visual and auditory tricks, and in no way prefiguring the kind of transcendent communication Ronni had referred to. But almost without trying, my thoughts began to diminish, or rather, I did not follow them along their normally anxious, questioning course. The barrier between sight and sound had been erased. I could no longer tell what was a result of the lights or the beats. Even more so than with the brain machine, this cross wiring of senses took hold. I could see/hear flaming mandalas forming and dissolving, the wash of the beats pouring through my body, the lights and colors pulsing out secret codes onto my mind's eye. I imagined for a moment that this was what we would perceive if Huxley's brain valve was permanently turned off. There was no tunnel pulling me down toward a new, unexplored realm as happened with the brain machine. This was more like I had turned on a television that was receiving signals directly from that other world. I didn't need to travel there out of my body.

The Dreamachine is a telescope—or a microscope, depending on what direction you want to imagine consciousness resides—and all I had to do was adjust my inner focus and not be afraid.

Over the course of all my explorations I have remained a skeptic, but have also become a sympathetic investigator of the supernatural and its technological manifestations. I could see now that there was more to find. I had felt the strange confluences of the occult and technology in the performance of magic, studied Shannon Taggart's photographs and seen more than coincidence, trod deeply into the uncanny valley with Nico Cox, listened for the voices of the dead with Donna Hogan, and even tried to build a golem. Armed with a soldering gun, a voltmeter, a few electronic components, and a computer with basic programming software, I was ready to take that leap to see what I might learn, and how what I might build could show me in what ways these current technologies and their antecedents shape our supernatural imaginations and our deepest desires that there is more to the universe than the physical.

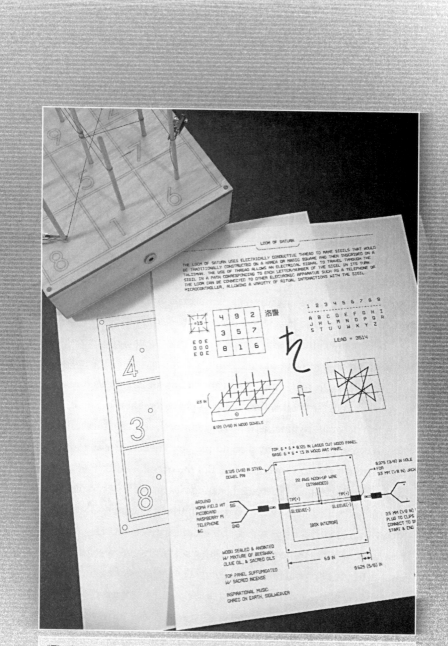

"The Loom of Saturn," a sigil-like device and schematic designed and built by Joshua Madara for ritual interactions

CHAPTER 7

Fear and Soldering

The parts list was simple enough: a coil, a diode, a nine-volt battery, a resistor, a ceramic capacitor, a small potentiometer, and a few feet of wire. Some soldering skill is required, but I have been building simple circuits since I was a kid. I had imagined the project would be easy, but I found that it was quite difficult making sense of what the device—known as a "spirit radio"—actually did. The project was posted on the website Instructables, one of the many online resources that is part of the DIY (do-it-yourself) renaissance and the maker movement. In an age of digital wonders, a new spirit of amateur invention—energized in part by the computer hacker Weltanschauung—is shaping the new millennium. Curious, then, that a device called the "Spooky Tesla Spirit Radio" should elicit dozens of comments in the post's thread, and reposts at websites like Gizmodo and *Make:* magazine. Embedded in this curious little Instructables project are a few remarkable outré trains of thought: a slightly conspiratorial idea of history where strange sciences are hidden from the masses and a persistent curiosity for how we might communicate with the dead (or other worlds) with simple electronic devices, both ideas that appeal to a DIY and hacker disposition. Certainly, as we have already seen, technology is not limited in its capacity to produce a sense of wonder and re-enchant the world. Despite well-established understandings of radio frequencies, including our ability to hear quasars and other phenomena in our solar system with a simple radio, the belief that the spirits of the dead or other entities might be able to communicate with us over a simple electronic circuit is just one aspect of a larger conception that has remained a fixed idea in the human imagination.

Many of these articles and blog posts written about the Instructables project quote from Nikola Tesla's 1901 diary entry where he writes, "My first observations positively terrified me as there was present in them something mysterious, not to say supernatural, and I was alone in my laboratory at night." It's a richly compelling image: the wide-eyed inventor, known to have an almost mystical, intuitive sense of electric currents and their behaviors, apprehended by a bizarre phenomenon. And although he is a scientist, he blinks and for a moment considers that there might be powers and forces beyond even his own superhuman comprehension.

The contraption is the simplest of its kind, essentially a crystal radio that is powered by electromagnetic waves. In 1899, Tesla was deep into his radio experiments, attempting to devise more powerful means of transmitting and receiving signals. By 1918, his experiments resulted in picking up sounds from all across the electromagnetic spectrum. In another diary entry, Tesla writes: "The sounds I am listening to every night at first appear to be human voices conversing back and forth in a language I cannot understand. I find it difficult to imagine that I am actually hearing real voices from people not of this planet. There must be a more simple explanation that has so far eluded me." For a time, Tesla thought the signals he was picking up from his radio were from Mars. As his equipment became more powerful, the voices coalesced into foreign languages. This didn't erase his vision for a future, however, where human beings and beings from other planets would one day form a spiritual union. In an interview with *TIME* in July of 1931, Tesla told the magazine, "I think that nothing can be more important than interplanetary communication. It will certainly come some day. And the certitude that there are other human beings in the universe . . . will produce a magic effect on mankind and will form the foundation of a universal brotherhood that will last as long as humanity itself." He had hoped he might build a device to make this possible, but admitted that his "physical powers" may not be sufficient for such a machine to be constructed.

Tesla himself is more legend than man. We live in a world made possible by his practical discoveries, including alternating current, but speculations of how far into the stratosphere his genius went perpetuated long after his death. His massive intellect would be credited to a kind of psychic faculty by his friend and biographer John J. O'Neill in his 1944 book *Prodigal Genius*, published a year after Tesla's death. O'Neill admits that Tesla eschewed any suggestion that there might be some truth to occult or paranormal phenomena, partly because he was worried such ideas would reduce him in the eyes of other scientists and the public. But O'Neill insists that Tesla had psychic powers, evidenced by having a number of premonitions including one about his mother's death. Tesla's own thoughts on the possibility of spiritual realities would take a decidedly skeptical turn when in his memoirs he would write, "I have proved to my complete satisfaction the automatism of life." But he would not give up on the idea that, as biographer Margaret

Cheney explains, there was still the possibility that there were some human beings who could be "sensitive receivers." This was not the result of any spiritual capacity, but rather that the person was akin to a sensitively tuned radio, picking up the intense feelings of others.

Conspiracy theories about Tesla abound. Secret experiments involving weapons, weather control, and, yes, devices for communicating with aliens would become as much a part of Tesla's legacy as his actual inventions. The alternative spiritual community known as Unarius, whose founder Ruth Norman is said to have channeled the extraterrestrial being known as Uriel, teaches that human beings are destined to be spiritually united with a vast interstellar brotherhood. Tesla is a kind of technological prophet, whom the Unarians deem has "Inner Perception or Cosmic Consciousness" and "will be known for the birthing of the New Age of Spiritual Renaissance on Earth!" (Exclamation theirs.)

These whimsical stories also uncover an important aspect of Tesla and why the radio project adheres so nicely to him and to the crosscurrents of the technological and spiritual imagination. Tesla was often considered an outsider, not bound by convention or even by the needs of the consumer and the market. This quality exposes what science historian W. Bernard Carlson explains as Tesla's other legacy, "that there is more to technology than relentless economic or scientific rationality." It is here that the ghost of Tesla guided my hand as I set out to build and experiment, and to see if I could wed the occult imagination with the technological within myself. Tesla, Carlson writes, "Created great technology by being in touch with his inner self, and he reveals that one can weave together the spiritual and the material."

At the heart of all the ways in which we have combined the supernatural quest with technology is the creative and the visionary, and even the more exaggerated and cartoonish expressions turn the same imaginary lock in our unconscious, a place where the spirit of Tesla often seems to have lodged. The linking of modern technology with arcane secrets would appear in multiple films and other media of the era in imaginative ways. In the mid-1960s, Stan Lee and Jack Kirby re-imagined Norse mythology for Marvel Comics, where Thor and other gods are more like interstellar beings who merge technology and magic. Kirby's illustrations here and in his later comics like *The New Gods* and *The Eternals* offered enormous techno-mystical machines and architecture that captured a vital aspect of how pop culture was shaping a new consciousness where machines and spiritual ideas could be linked. These were all stories and images of cosmic gods and alien avatars. Back on Earth, we could write them into fiction, but waiting for them to deliver us to a technological new age wouldn't do. We had to be the agents of any human eschaton worth believing in. On the other side of the Atlantic, the BBC televised *The Stone Tapes* in 1972, the story of a group of electronic and computer engineers who take up residence in an old Victorian mansion hoping to invent a new kind of recording medium. Strange goings-on begin to suggest the house is haunted, but the engineers soon discover the very stones of the building have "recorded" the history of the home, one filled with trauma and violence. Once human ingenuity and inventiveness became intimately tied into our technological prowess, what had once been thought of as miraculous could be easily rendered as merely another human-engineered apparatus, like one of Tesla's dramatic electrically flowering coils.

It was out of this historical and cultural milieu—psychedelic visions of the future and ghost-haunted televisions—that my own occult imagination was born, and so I drilled, wound wire, soldered—during which I burned the tip of my finger—and when I was done, I found that I was obsessively fine-tuning the little radio expecting I, too, would hear the message that, for example, drove Roy Neary in *Close Encounters of the Third Kind* toward his transcendent fate. The radio produced very little in the way of otherworldly effects. I tried to increase the levels of what the radio picked up by recording its output into my computer, amplifying the sounds with audio software, and keeping my eye out for spikes in the waveforms and then reamplifying those areas. I picked up a few clips of noise and a stray hum here and there, but nothing in the way of voices. My intention to hear spirits or otherworldly sounds had brought me into communion with the very visionary quest I have been exploring up to this point, so much so that when my radio failed to produce any noise other than static, I was disappointed. Whatever core skepticism I had was rendered inert by the process of building. I was willing to entertain the idea that I might encounter a phenomenon that could be perceived as supernatural, at least in quality, if not origin. Tied into this supernatural expedition was that I was working outside the accepted scientific rubric of how radios function and the very nature of frequencies. Even asking the question as to whether or not a small crystal radio can pick up signals from other worlds is a kind of rational heresy. Using my father's reel-to-reel also ignited this similarly irrational part of my imagination, but the act of building, of making a device whose intent is at odds with its known function, situated itself within a current that has always moved parallel to that of the technological investigations into the supernatural. I had, in effect, become a hacker and a maker, a participant in the inventive momentum that has driven all technological progress.

Underneath the hacker ethos is the organizing vision called cyberculture, and the cyberpunk fiction that inspired it, which Gareth Branwyn called, in part, a rejection of the organic and magical thinking of 1960s/1970s counterculture. "Where that culture had been sensual and earthy, cyberculture was all mental and technological," Gareth explained to me over e-mail. "The body became 'the meat,' little more than a home for the brain, and whatever hedonistic pleasures the meat might provide." But as Gareth noted, even cyberpunk couldn't keep the spiritual out of the digital. The novelist William Gibson, known for his influential novel *Neuromancer*, continued to build his cyberculture society in his follow-up book, *Count Zero*, where he introduces artificial intelligences that adopt the names and attributes of the Loa, the gods of Haitian Vodou. The practical, results-based magic of Voudon helped inspire the creation of "chaos magick," what Gareth called one of the dominant faiths of 1990s cyberculture.

Media theorist Steve Collins explains that all magic shares a hacker element: "In the instance of hacking, it is the underlying code that must be altered to exert a change; for magic, it is the manipulation of forces underpinning the state of existence that brings about change." When envisaged through this lens, all of the technological encounters that I have had so far have been imagination hacks, breaking open the rational and mussing around with the wiring to create new systems of thought that adhere to the irrational. It's just a matter of keeping the virus scanners turned off, those skeptical bots that scour my consciousness zapping any attempt to repurpose my mind's conditioned way of thinking. Whether during the perceptional shift that occurs when engaging with Shannon Taggart's haunted photographs, stepping off the cliff into the uncanny valley of Nico's automatons, contemplating my golem, or fearfully hoping to hear a spirit on the reel-to-reel recorder, in all these instances some measure of a hack is taking place. In these cases, the hack was involuntary. The feelings of enchantment and wonder arose from the outside stimulus. By sitting down to build a device whose purpose is to activate the irrational, I am deliberately attempting to hack my imagination. I might be accused of doing nothing more than self-suggesting, opening a placebo wormhole where what I expect to encounter will be likely to occur in my interpretations, along the spectrum of what Joe Banks describes in *Rorschach Audio*, noted earlier. I would argue it is more a form of role-playing, where building and making—where hacking—aligns me with both the form and substance of the belief in the supernatural that originally drove the ideas in the first place. My little Tesla radio was only getting me so far, though. I needed to build a more potent device.

In 1995, the October issue of *Popular Electronics* offered the article "Ghost Voices: Exploring the Mysteries of Electronic Voice Phenomena (EVP)," and laid out a few methods for modifying radios to be able to answer whether "the dead are trying to break through the veil between the worlds." Various techniques are presented: a simple tape recorder with a microphone in a quiet room might record answers to questions that can be heard on playback (tried it, no luck); a circuit to build a small radio much like the Tesla radio I built; tuning a radio between stations and recording the static; and a white noise generator schematic to use instead of a radio to be sure stray transmissions are not being picked up. The tone of the piece is playful but not skeptical. The author takes no position, but *Popular Electronics* was written for the amateur hobbyist, and if any audience would be interested in such an article, it would certainly be this magazine's readers.

After the article was published, the magazine was overwhelmed with letters, and in the 1996 February edition, the editors published a number of examples. They range from rational insight ("The 'voices of the dead' theme is simply an example of the phenomenon known to engineers as audio rectification"), outrage ("This is indeed a low point for the . . . magazine"), and cautious belief ("I think that the EVP is something that can't be explained away"). But the letter from C.W. from Lee's Summit, Missouri, is the most revealing. The writer concurs that electronic hobbyists are "different from others because . . . we are curious about physical phenomena. We seek to know more and more about the physical nature of our universe. The article provides us with a means to delve into another aspect of our universe, namely the spiritual." Rather than amaze the editors with their experiments, the letter instead issues a stern warning. "Do not communicate with the dead," C.W. writes, "for it is written in Deuteronomy 18:10–12: 'There shall not be found among you anyone that . . . useth divination, or an observer of times, or an enchanter, or a witch, or a charmer, or a consuler of familiar spirits, or a wizard, or a necromancer.'" It's no surprise that a letter to the editor in an electronics hobby magazine would illuminate the tension at the heart of both the occult and the inventive spirit.

The occult, understood to be a set of spiritual and magical practices that are often at odds with normative religious customs, rarely aligns with the mainstream American ideal of the individual as a frontiersman, exploring the limits of what is possible in an effort to build and expand outward into the antipodes. Technology is also often at odds with religious values as well because similarly it places too much power in the hands of the human being, leaving little room for God. But, unlike the occult, technological innovation more readily can be understood as being a gift from God, a measure of salvation and the perfection of the soul. When we combine technology with the spiritual even when outside of accepted religious practice, the edges begin to blur. It becomes a realm not accepted by either religious traditionalist or scientists. The hobbyist, with a DIY engine in their heart, has always propelled these kinds of activities forward.

Frank Sumption, a ham radio enthusiast, was one of the many readers of the *Popular Electronics* article, and had always harbored an interest in the paranormal. He tried some of the experiments, and according to his friend Tim Woolworth—author of the blog ITC Voices—Frank wasn't impressed with the results. But in 2000, Frank tried again, this time going outside of the projects offered in the magazine. Spirits, according to EVP experimenters, cannot communicate in a vacuum. Bound—in some uncategorical way—by the laws of physics, spirits require a carrier of some kind to transmit their voices into our world. When a digital FM radio is set to scan, it "locks" as soon as it receives a strong frequency. Frank discovered that by modifying a radio so that it never locks on a station, the resulting effect is a constant stream of noise, bits of music, voices, and static. This raw material, Sumption claimed, could be used by spirits to form words. "It's been my experience that if one supplies something that the spirits/entities can use to make voices out of," he wrote, "'they' will speak." The hacked radios came to be affectionately known within the EVP community as "Frank Boxes."

Sumption's experiments would take a strange turn. First, he became increasingly irritated by the people claiming to be ghost hunters. He started to assert that the voices he was receiving might be alien in nature. In an e-mail correspondence with the writer Karen Stollznow, Sumption explained that the entities he spoke with believed that he was a missing intergalactic royal lady who they called the "purple princess." His boxes also became more sophisticated, and he eventually created a version with a small CRT screen in an attempt to pick up images of the entities he was in communication with.

Sumption's original ghost box has since been modified by others using the most recent electronic hobbyist technologies, such as microcontrollers—small programmable devices that allow simple circuits to be easily hacked together and improved upon without having to change the primary circuit. Computer programming has essentially altered the basic design of the spirit radio in such a way that a once purely analog device—little more than a coil picking up stray frequencies (and possibly a disembodied soul)—has become a digital node in the vast, and seemingly infinite, cyberspace. Software code is shared; EVP samples are uploaded to YouTube. The devices themselves are hooked up to personal computers, creating a virtual web of receivers drawing down these noises. My experiences with computer-based applications led me to become distrustful of methods whose designs are hidden. But it was not only that these digital ghost boxes could be fraudulent; they don't allow for the inventive experimental character of something like Frank Sumption's boxes. The supernatural imagination demands a special kind of activation, one that often requires breaking radios and making them do something they weren't intended to do but are more than capable of doing.

EVP hobbyists are particularly fond of RadioShack digital radios for their ease of opening and rewiring, but they are unfortunately no longer produced. Trying to procure one was daunting. I scoured Goodwill and other local thrift shops but was unable to find one that was included on various EVP "hackable" lists. A search on eBay returned only a few hits, most of which were upward of a hundred dollars. One that had been "prehacked" started at $225. Most listings don't promise that the buyer will actually hear spirits, but a recent listing confided that "At the cemetery or at my house it was getting great replies," and linked to a website with video evidence of the radio in use. I was intent on building one myself, and so I patiently checked eBay listings until I finally procured a RadioShack model 12-589 "Extreme-Range AM/FM Weather

Radio" in working condition. Its only flaw was a broken antenna, which was easily replaced. There was something satisfying about it being a RadioShack radio. The company once had a reputation for being hobbyist friendly, and I myself have a long history with them. My first electronics kit was their "150 in 1 Project Kit," and the first thing I ever soldered was a small multitester from their line of kits known as ArcherKit. I also worked for RadioShack in my early twenties when the stores were still the go-to shop for electronic tinkerers. I had grown up in and around RadioShacks, and there would be nothing more natural than taking a screwdriver to the case screws of one of their radios, opening it up, and mucking around with the circuit. I was in unfamiliar territory making a ghost box, but with an intimately familiar map.

The website Keyport Paranormal offers a set of instructions, written by the website's creator, Steve Hultay, for using the model 12-589. It requires breaking the radio so it continually scans even when a clear signal is found, and building a small operational amplifier that is used to speed up the scanning. Once the hack was complete, I set up the radio on my desk, turned on a handheld digital recorder, powered up the radio, and set it to scan. Most practitioners suggest the sessions be limited to five minutes. It was also important for me to remember that these devices are intended to facilitate communication. They are not simply picking up stray signals from the spirit world, but acting as two-way transmitters. So instead of just listening, I asked a series of questions. When I turned on the radio and began to scan, I realized that my radio was not performing as the instructions laid out. To limit the amount of words and bits of songs that are picked up with a scan at normal rate, the voltage needs to be changed to speed up the sweep so that when functioning, the sounds should be almost unintelligible, limiting how often clear words are heard. It took me a few tries to get the circuit working correctly, but eventually, my radio was sweeping the frequencies at a much more rapid pace.

To add a bit more atmosphere and to give my imagination a little boost as well, I turned to the most popular depiction of ghost hunting with homemade electronics, the 1984 film *Ghostbusters*. In particular, the psychokinetic energy (PKE) meter invented by the character Dr. Egon Spengler, was what I wanted to try and replicate. The device, as shown in the film, registers ghostly activity by picking up oscillations in the electromagnetic field. As it turns out, this kind of device, called an EMF meter, is a primary tool of amateur ghost hunters. There are many EMF meter plans online, and I found one using the Arduino brand of programmable microcontroller. Instead of having to build a complicated circuit, with a few simple parts and some code uploaded to the Arduino from my laptop, I had a working EMF meter in a few minutes. On a small solderless breadboard (a prototyping tool used for experimenting with electronic circuit designs before committing them to solder), I hooked up a red LED, a resistor, and a small piece of insulated wire with an inch of insulation removed. The LED pulsed as I walked around my house with the circuit, getting brighter and more stable near electrical outlets and other electronic devices.

The discovery of electromagnetic fields was quickly associated with a spirit medium's ability. Because we live in a physical world, denizens of the spirit world would need some kind of natural force to cross over to our realm. The first idea came by way of Franz Mesmer's formulation of animal magnetism described earlier, which would become one of the ways of explaining—in rational terms—the relationship between the medium and the spirits. Mediums were particularly sensitive, it was thought, to the magnetic fluids that surround us. In the early twentieth century, Oliver Lodge, a physicist and Spiritualist, argued that spirits existed within a pervasive substance through which the electromagnetic field could move which he called the ether. The historian Jenny Hazelgrove writes that it was supposed that "[Ether] fused the physical plane with the metaphysical realm and promised to be the basis of a moral and teleological account of existence." Eventually the notion of an ether was discounted, but the belief that spirits rode along or beside electromagnetic fields was fixed. It wasn't much of a leap to imagine that if spirits did indeed share certain frequencies with this invisible spectrum, then they could be measured.

I turned on my digital recorder, pressed the "scan" button on the radio, and then invited any spirits or entities in, telling them I was a curious and open-minded friend. After a few moments, I asked a series of questions: Is there anyone here? Can you tell me your name? Do you have any messages for me? I wasn't expecting to hear anything right away. And given how quickly the radio was sweeping frequencies, it was difficult to make out anything clearly. At one point I heard the word "skeleton." I asked if they had said "skeleton," and almost immediately the word was repeated. I then asked, "What do you want to say about skeletons?" I couldn't be sure if I had even heard the word correctly. Most EVP results, it is believed, are better heard during playback. A small bit of the audio caught my attention, but I couldn't make out the words. Using the audio editing software, I cut out the section, amplified it, and slowed it down. "Maybe we can help you," the voice said.

The simplest explanation is that someone on one of the radio stations being picked up in the scanning was talking about skeletons and I was simply picking up traces. But while the word itself had no direct meaning for me, it is certainly one that evokes a creepy unease. Here I was trying to capture a voice from the dead, and the one clear word was "skeleton." One of the difficulties with using a device like this is that there is so much noise and so many random phrases it's difficult to discern any kind of meaning from the sweep. Frustrated with what is supposed to be a surefire way to trigger electronic voice phenomenon, I wrote to Steve Hultay, whose ghost box design I was using, to get some advice. It largely comes down to experience, he told me. Years of doing EVP research is what he believes makes him able to pick out distinct voices. He also tries to limit what he calls "false positives," the stray bits of voices being broadcast. Steve has gone so far as to design ghost boxes that broadcast reverse speech so that any discernible words have more likelihood of being EVPs.

Even when successful with what might appear like true EVPs, the question of the source remains one of the questions that the community cannot agree on. Raudive never hesitated to say the voices he collected were spirits of the dead, but even the father of EVP is considered quaint these days. Not only has the technology advanced far beyond Raudive's analog tape recorders, the UFO culture has changed the conversation entirely. While there remains a slightly Christian flavor to much of the EVP world (even Steve told me the voices might "be lower-level spirits pretending to be our long-lost loved ones, for all we know") there is a subgroup of enthusiasts who believe the EVPs are extraterrestrial (echoing Tesla, who thought the voices he picked up might be Martian) or even interdimensional. The notion of interdimensional entities tracks more readily to the original EVP accounts by Jürgenson and Raudive as they can be linked to the history of supernatural occurrences. John Keel, best known as the author of the cryptozoology classic *The Mothman Prophecies*, warned in his 1970 book *Operation Trojan*

Horse that we were being manipulated by alien entities into believing they were extraterrestrial, when in fact they are malevolent supernatural entities, "from some other space-time continuum."

This idea is supported, albeit less ominously, by the great UFO scholar and researcher Jacques Vallée and the inspiration for the French ufologist Claude Lacombe, played by François Truffaut in Steven Spielberg's 1977 film *Close Encounters of the Third Kind*. It was *Close Encounters* that introduced a wider audience to an alien intelligence that might come to Earth not to conquer but to transfigure human consciousness. In the 1950s, the alien—often said to be from Mars—was a stand-in for Communist invaders, as in the 1956 film *Invasion of the Body Snatchers*. And while otherworldly visitors sometimes came with benevolent intent, such as Klaatu from *The Day the Earth Stood Still*, even there the threat of destruction was still in the cards if we didn't behave ourselves. But Steven Spielberg's operatic vision of advanced technology and spiritual transformation completely rewrote UFO mythology.

In *Close Encounters*, Roy Neary (Richard Dreyfuss) and Jillian Guiler (Melinda Dillon) are each implanted with a psychic message after having had an "encounter" with alien ships and are compelled to be at the arrival coordinates the government has worked so hard to hide. After a nail-biting escape from army helicopters dropping sleeping gas to prevent them from reaching the landing site, Neary rushes into the crowd of scientists and military personnel to get close to the enormous city-sized mothership that descends from an almost religious vision of clouds parting. The ship opens and a group of abductees from various points in twentieth-century history disembarks the mothership as if in a kind of trance. We can only assume their experience has elevated them to something more than human. Soon after, tiny wide-eyed benevolent aliens emerge, milling around until they settle on Neary, like curious children. They hold his arms aloft and then lead him onto the ship. The door closes, and the vessel ascends back into the heavens, a technological rapture in which the human being, Neary, will be transfigured. The spiritual ascension seen in *Close Encounters* was possible because the scientists and other researchers teased out the meaning behind the musical notes their communication was based on: coordinates for the landing site of the enormous mothership. Here is a fundamental idea embedded in the EVP subculture: we had to meet the mystery of the universe halfway. If they called, we had to be ready to answer.

Close Encounters drew from a well of actual untested theories and beliefs that extraterrestrial superscience was being used for metaphysical purpose. Alongside the alien-as-invader motif seen in many films of that time, alternative religious communities were forming, with their own unique visions of alien visitation. As early as 1954, George King—a British Quaker and yoga practitioner—announced that he had been contacted telepathically by Master Aetherius from the planet Venus, who told King that he had been chosen to become "the voice of Interplanetary Parliament." King is said to have channeled hundreds of messages from extraterrestrial intelligences—spiritual masters—who wanted to teach human beings how to activate their spiritual potential. That same year, the aircraft mechanic George Van Tassel—drawing on what he believed was the architectural model for Moses's tabernacle in the desert as well as telepathic communication from aliens—built a round dome-like structure called the Integratron out in the Mojave Desert. Tassel believed that by utilizing and focusing certain electromagnetic fields, the Integratron could revive damaged cells in the human body, potentially offering extended life and health. The Integratron is still with us, now offering a sensory "Sound Bath," in which visitors can sit in the dome as crystal bowls are "played," producing healing and meditative effects. Along this spectrum from religious communities to popular films like *Close Encounters*, significant numbers of folks shared stories of abductions by aliens, all of it morphing into the culturally acceptable notion that alien technology had spiritual implications: our human destiny is not simply to visit other worlds, but to walk among the stars as gods.

Vallée, who has said he never was committed to the belief that UFOs are extraterrestrial in origin, in 1988 published *Dimensions*, a book in which he argues that many alien abduction stories are eerily similar to historical sightings of divine beings such as angels, fairies, and demons. Vallée makes the significant point that in the long history of UFO and abduction accounts, the aliens never make direct contact with a person of considerable influence or in a manner that is direct and verifiable: "They did not speak to our scientists; they did not send sophisticated signals in uniquely decipherable codes as any well-behaved alien should before daring to penetrate our solar system." Instead, they contact and abduct farmers, ordinary couples driving home at night, and other regular people, and indeed their stories read like encounters with strange beings that have been with us for centuries, particularly those found in folklore. After documenting dozens of contemporary reports and their antecedents in myth and legends, Vallée proposes that, rather than being from outer space, if otherworldly visitors are real, it is more likely "the phenomenon could be a manifestation of a much more complex technology" that can manipulate both space and time. Echoing the work of Robert Monroe, whose writings on out-of-body experiences argue that our consciousness can leave our bodies, Vallée suggests this might be the technique used by these other dimensional beings.

It becomes much more interesting, then, to think about a ghost box as a consciousness radio rather than a receiver for spirits of the dead. Just as Shannon Taggart deliberately plays with accident and chance, the ghost box experience is one that acts like Shannon's camera. Instead of imposing the elements of chance when listening to a ghost box, the device is creating these conditions. It is also possible to imagine that the listener is the subject, not the voices. Our own consciousness becomes a kind of canvas for these voices—call them spirits if you want—to draw or write whatever messages we are able to process. Think of a ghost box like an electronic tarot deck or the roll of an I Ching hexagram. The ghost box is just as well a tool for divination, as opposed to communication. Sweeping across radio bands, it acts as an audio version of a Ouija board.

Part of the divinatory quality of the ghost box arises out of the concept of the "glitch." A glitch occurs when there is some failure in a system, often one that is intended to produce clean output. Stray signals from a radio picked up by a baby monitor, pixelated artifacts in a video game, or an error in a digital audio file are all glitches. Electronic musician and composer Kim Cascone explains that our instincts are to either dismiss or fix these glitches, but we should instead look to them as opportunities for spiritual and creative insight. In his essay "Errormancy," Kim writes that for a particularly deft artist "a glitch can form a brief rupture in the space-time continuum, shuffling the psychic space of the observer, allowing the artist to establish a direct link with the supernal realm." This is, as we saw, the very definition of the most common form of divination known as cleromancy. A set of objects—cards, bones, coins, dice—is shuffled or tossed, and the chance results are read in the hopes that they reveal some important understanding of a problem or future situation, or act as a mirror for a current psychological state.

Over e-mail, I asked Kim if he agreed that EVP could be used as a form of cleromancy. "In the right hands, any technology can be used as a divination tool," he wrote, but he agrees that when EVP technology is used to hunt for ghosts, the amount of expectation built in means that "human bias is loaded into the experience," something he also thinks is true with a device like a Ouija board. Kim believes that divination, particularly when done with technology, should only be attempted when the person has first done their own inner spiritual work. At one time, divination was the purview of the shaman or the soothsayer, a person who was thought to be chosen by the gods to act as an intermediary between the two worlds. But as Christianity ascended, particularly in the pagan world, it was left to the common people to do their own divination. And it often had to be done in secret. This created an oral tradition that no longer relied on a certain person within the community to do divination work. Nevertheless, Kim sees that there was a certain truth to being spiritually attuned for divination to be truly efficacious. Otherwise, as Kim says, "the whole thing is nothing more than a mirror of our own projections." This is, of course, exactly where much of the EVP culture breaks down as Joe Banks demonstrates in *Rorschach Audio*. The danger to self-deception, especially in matters related to the supernatural, links all the technology being explored thus far. Kim's advice regarding using EVP in the same ways as something like the I Ching requires that a ghost box become a "silent channel." Most experiments with EVP rely partly on conscious listening, inspecting every spike of sound or anomaly on the recordings hoping to hear something unexplainable. By allowing the technology to disappear into the background, Kim writes, one lets their own intuition be the guide. For divination to work, Kim believes, "technology must become invisible to the user and a Zen-like detachment be practiced."

What Kim is proposing effectively gets at the tension that sits at the heart of how technology and the occult work together. Sometimes the technology is hidden as in the case of Pepper's Ghost or Roberts's phantasmagoria performances. In other cases, the technology completes the circuit in our imaginations, such as spirit photography or EVPs. Ferdinando Buscema's performances use literal technology like the Llullian wheel and an iPhone, but the "trick" is hidden. Joshua Madara's magic purposely uses electronics to assist in his magical practice. And then there are the automata, whose uncanniness sits at the location where the clockwork is hidden but presupposed. In all cases, however, the device or machine is what activates the imagination.

On a far spectrum from Kim, who sees technology as a potential stopgap to the experience, Madara offered to teach me some experiments using computers in a way that requires them to be very much a part of the interface between the person and whatever kind of divinatory message might be perceived. A few weeks after he offered to help, Joshua sent me an e-mail with a link to a password-protected website, a work in progress called Technomancy 101, where I would be taught the secrets of electronic divination, conjuration, and invocation. It felt as though I had been accepted into a magical lodge, an invitation from a secret Rosicrucian order that had decided I was ready to be instructed in the arcane arts.

Many of the projects require working with the graphical programming language Scratch, one of Joshua's primary tools in his magical arsenal. "One of the earliest uses of the computer in art was randomness.

Anything that involves a set of tokens that is randomized, computers do that really well," he told me. One of Joshua's projects is called Scrycloud, built using Scratch. Scratch uses "sprites"—pregenerated objects that can be used to perform various functions. A sprite can be animated, used as a simple graphical representation such as an on/off button, or simply for aesthetics. To program Scratch, you place colored command blocks on top of each other, building your project as you go, rather than coding line by line. The Scrycloud program is designed by first choosing a background image, a sigil or other symbol, and then layering over it with three other images with seven variations textured with imaging software to look like clouds. The Scratch code tells the cloud sprites to randomly cycle. Along with the shifting clouds, Joshua added a looping ambient soundtrack. When the program runs, the user stares into the screen, watching as the shifting clouds seem to morph as sigil flutters, appearing and disappearing into the noise. It's a bit like looking into an old black-and-white TV tuned to an unused channel, but the addition of the sigil creates an illusion of other solid forms warping and weaving within the static.

The psychological effect at play is known as pareidolia, where the mind is able to take random patterns in sights and sounds and order them into recognizable features, such as seeing animal shapes in clouds or hearing devilish messages in albums played backward. Pareidolia is the phenomenon that allows someone to hear words form in the quickly scanning noises of a ghost box. Pareidolia also has a long spiritual and religious significance, as many reported sightings of Jesus, Mary, and other saints occurring on the surface of other objects. Believers have discovered divine imagery in the grains of a piece of wood, on a stained cloth, and even on a piece of toast. One of the more remarkable examples is found in a photograph taken by the Hubble Space Telescope.

Many people have seen in the cone nebula image a silhouette of the popular conceptions of Jesus, long hair and beard raining down with bright stars forming a kind of halo around his head. The context lends cosmic significance as well. And like the YouTube videos of subtitled EVPs, it becomes almost impossible to not see the figure of Jesus when viewing the photo once you know others have seen it.

I decided to make some changes to Joshua's version of the Scrycloud by using the medieval magical seal called the Sigillum Dei, or Seal of God, inscribed by John Dee on a stone and kept on the altar while he used one of his scrying crystals. The seal is made up of heptagrams surrounded by two sets of symbols with a pentagram in the center for good measure and adorned with the names of angels and variations on the name of God, such as "El." The Sigillum perfectly embodies centuries of magical practice, and is situated at a time when the magic of divination was considered natural and rational, as in the work of Giambattista della Porta. My choice of the Sigillum, however, was a bit superficial. While I liked the idea that this was the symbol that adorned one of Dee's shew stones and retains its history, it's an oddly potent mirror of my own occult imagination, kindling deep nostalgia for everything from Dungeons & Dragons to paperback occult novels. The Sigillum's ability to quickly activate that part of my unconscious also speaks to how there is an inherent quality to certain images and symbols that quickens that part of ourselves that immediately recognizes their occult resonances, even when we don't believe they reference any reality beyond our own.

Staring into the cloudy Sigillum was like looking back to the very earliest moments when I was taken in by supernatural and otherworldly narratives like *Poltergeist* and *Close Encounters of the Third Kind*. But these are also archetypes, ancient codes written so deeply into our psychic DNA that it's impossible to have an encounter of this kind that is not informed by them. Staring at the Scrycloud, I can divine not only my own deep history with D&D magic-users launching fireballs, magical grimoires sold at mall bookstores, and the moment Indy shields his eyes from the destructive, divine magic of the Ark of the Covenant, but I am also witnessing something far older, numinous even. Two essential points converge. To divine on a computer, using code that I could see, understand, and repurpose is magic in its most direct form. The world of the spirit, however it might exist, expands into view when I activate my own creative and inventive capacities.

When I began this adventure, I first imagined I might build a golem, the most analog of all magical technologies. My final effort finds me programming ones and zeroes to create a digital reflection of my own supernatural curiosity. Just as in the kabbalist tradition, where the golem marked the mystic's power and specialness, Kevin LaGrandeur notes, our technology has become the domain of an extraordinary kind of wisdom; scientists and coders are the new wizards. "They're the magicians of our age," he told me by phone. Coders, for example, call the background programs that run behind the operating system on a computer "daemons," benevolent guardian spirits that act as invisible helpers. So I have taken the clay and added the secret names, and what I have found is that Rabbi Eyal Riess was right all along: the golem reflects my own spiritual and supernatural unconsciousness, built from the ground up by a lifetime of occult and supernatural images and ideas that are a deep part of my psyche, carved there by religion, pop culture, and personal interest, as well as ancient archetypes that are programmed into all of us.

I asked Joshua the question that had been at the root of my explorations: Why has technology not pulled us completely away from the magical? "For me," he answered, "it's really about that notion of enchantment." Joshua uses the example of his own work. A person viewing it can analyze the technique and the materials. They might even be able to reverse engineer the effects if they recognize the basic elements being used, such as an LED connected to a microcontroller. But what they cannot easily replicate is what Joshua calls the "gooey, uncertain" feeling that the work evokes. Where does the intention of the work arise? No amount of technical know-how can reproduce the enchantment without it. What the device or ritual evokes in the audience remains part of the mystery we have been witnessing here from the start. The sense of the numinous is what happens in the interaction. This is the location where the magician, the artist, and the hacker meet.

The systems in place to build machines will say that the device is intended for a specific purpose. A radio is made for the express purpose of tuning in to certain frequencies across the radio wave spectrum and then amplifying them. But the hacker, particularly a mischievous one, who Joshua calls "the mercurial hacker," will expose the hidden complexity by repurposing the radio, by getting it to do something that the inventor of the machine or the typical user does not see or believe in. In fact, the hacker might also try to increase or reinsert what the original maker had tried to reduce or eliminate altogether. The hacker reminds us, Joshua contends, that although our model of the world is stable and organized, there always exists the potential for it to be different. When we are made aware of this, there is the possibility to reshape our imaginations, and in effect, alter our consciousness.

A state of altered consciousness, no matter how it is achieved, has transformative potential. Once we become open to mystery, we can recognize other moments when the word of the spirit—even if wholly imagined—enters us. In his book *The Trickster and the Paranormal*,

George Hansen makes the point that the very nature of supernatural phenomena—what he calls its trickster quality—makes it particularly susceptible to fraudulence, and yet it continues to exert a powerful influence over our culture. Technology provides a means to investigate this tension, offering tools that allow us to exert control over our imaginations in the same way that ritual and performance can deepen our ability to gaze into the unknown and be astonished. All magic then becomes a method of hacking systems. This is also what Shannon Taggart does, for example, with her photography. The reality of the medium just sitting in a chair is hacked so that a one-minute exposure completely changes everything you thought you knew about that moment when you look at the image later.

I have been arguing thus far that using technology toward some occult or supernatural purpose is not only an extension of our innate desire to master our own spiritual destiny, but has been a means to re-enchant the world even as it seems to move further toward a wholly rational technological future. Moreover, by using certain devices such as a Dreamachine, we can create states of wonder that expose our supernatural and occult imaginations. But any method that can increase these perceptions can literally change the way our brains work. In their book *Supernatural as Natural*, professors John Baker and Michael Winkelman invert Robert Monroe and others' idea that alpha waves can bridge supernatural realities by demonstrating that supernatural and magical rituals can themselves produce alpha wave states. They describe the example of the indigenous tribal shaman whose frenetic movements by way of dance, drumming, and shouting can place them into a semiconscious but hyperaware state of mind. Moreover, those witnessing the performance, or even viewing a symbolic representation of the shaman's journey to the spirit world in the form of paintings, can be induced to experience similar brain wave activity. As we have seen, technology can be used to create supernatural resonances as well as to act as a medium for imagining we are communicating with other realms. Like the occult imagination, which involves all our hopes and fears related to the supernatural and magic, technology provides a literal mechanism for altering our perceptions or for demanding that we perceive something in a new way. We live deeply in the midst of a culture of science and innovation that doesn't leave much room for superstition and belief in magic. The almost divine irony is that technology has actually allowed us to witness the fact that the spiritual world is not completely cut off from the material.

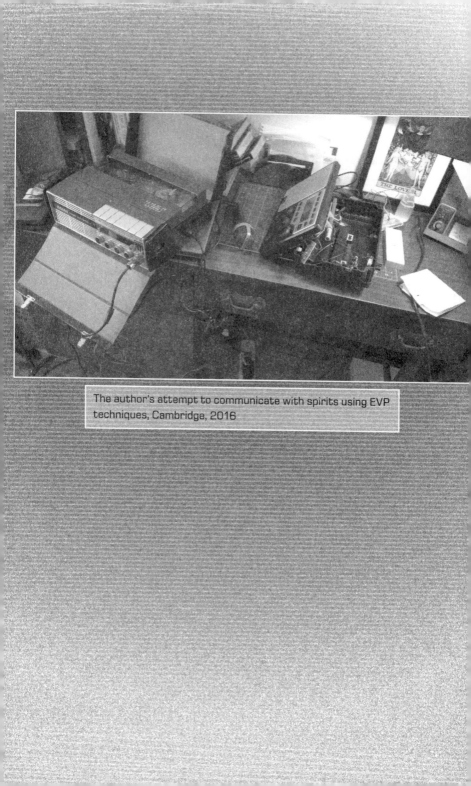

The author's attempt to communicate with spirits using EVP techniques, Cambridge, 2016

POSTSCRIPT

My desk is littered with electronic parts, broken radios, tape recorders, and old computers. With the DIY hacker sensibility at my heels and a lifetime of occult resonances, I have soldered, programmed, repurposed, and then activated my projects. I used computers to divine, built an automaton, listened over and over to tiny pieces of recordings trying to tease out a message from the dead or some other supernatural entity. I even invited the spirit of my father—whose voice in my head underpinned my skeptical thoughts—to communicate with me through his old reel-to-reel recorder. In all these efforts, I exposed myself to ideas that had shot through the history of technology from the beginning, when magic and science were believed to be aspects of the same universal laws. I felt the desire of the Spiritualists whose own need for evidence of life after death might have even confused their own ability to discern truth from fancy. Like magic and ritual, technology has long been understood as another tool for connecting to the divine and enacting our will upon nature. Of course, technology has been used to trick others into believing in the existence of divine and supernatural powers as well as by those who seek to demonstrate the supposed falsity of these beliefs. But even for those who will use technology toward a more skeptical purpose, they nevertheless inspire and ignite the occult imagination.

One night, I was working with my father's old Uher recorder, going through the old reels that had been packed up along with the recorder when we were moving things out of my father's house in the days after he died. One of the tapes was labeled "Moody's Mood for Love," a recording from 1956 by the jazz singer Eddie Jefferson. One side was the album that my father recorded from his turntable, but the other side was my mother, then twenty-four years old, singing along to other records playing in the background. She must have been holding the very microphone that I was using for my experiments as I tried to capture the sounds of spirits. Her voice was not great, but she meant it, singing her heart out into the recorder. My son was in the room when I was listening to the tape. They had never met, and he had never heard her voice, having been born a few years after she passed away. I watched him, quietly astonished as my mother's voice rose up out of the speakers, her spirit filling the room. Here indeed was the voice of the dead coming from the ether through this electronic device. We were hearing a ghost speak. I had put skepticism aside, hoping with dread that I might hear the voice of my deceased father. Instead, my mother had paid a visit from the past, and I was haunted in a way far deeper.

Notes on Sources

INTRODUCTION: "IT'S A TRANSMITTER!
A RADIO FOR SPEAKING TO GOD!"

Quotes from *New York Times* article from John Noble Wilford's "Men Walk on Moon," *New York Times*, July 21, 1969: 1.

History of television and quote by Jeffrey Sconce from his book *Haunted Media: Electronic Presence from Telegraphy to Television*, Durham, NC: Duke University Press, 2000.

Material from the first 1968 edition of the *Whole Earth Catalog* are from digital reprints found at http://www.wholeearth.com.

Louis Agassiz quote from his *An Essay on Classification*, Cambridge: Belknap Press of Harvard University Press, 1962.

Quotes from Harry Truman's speech found at "Harry S. Truman: Statement by the President Announcing the Use of the A-Bomb at Hiroshima," http://www.presidency.ucsb.edu/ws/?pid=12169.

CHAPTER 1: THE GOLEM OF BOSTON

I. L. Peretz's golem story found in "The Golem," Irving Howe and Eliezer Greenberg, eds., *A Treasury of Yiddish Stories*, New York: Schocken, 1973.

Everything you need to know about my adolescent psyche is found in Gary Gygax's *Advanced Dungeons & Dragons Monster Manual*, Lake Geneva, WI: TSR

Hobbies, 1978, and *Advanced Dungeons & Dragons Dungeon Masters Guide*, Lake Geneva, WI: TSR Games, 1979.

Quote from the Talmud found at the excellent online resource, "Babylonian Talmud: Sanhedrin 65," http://www.come-and-hear.com/sanhedrin/sanhedrin_65.html#65b_23.

Information on the golem and Jakob Grimm found in Edan Dekel and David Gantt Gurley's "How the Golem Came to Prague," *The Jewish Quarterly Review* 103, no. 2 (Spring 2013): 241–258.

Quotes from Mark Podwal's essential golem story from his book *Golem: A Giant Made of Mud*, New York: Greenwillow Books, 1995.

Quotes from the *Sefer Yetzirah* from two different sources, first from Aryeh Kaplan's masterful *Sefer Yetzirah: The Book of Creation*, 2nd revised edition, York Beach, ME: Weiser Books, 1997, and the invaluable online resource "Sefaria: A Living Library of Jewish Text," found at https://www.sefaria.org/.

The two most important texts on the golem for this work are Moshe Idel's *Golem: Jewish Magical and Mystical Traditions on the Artificial Anthropoid*, Albany: State University of New York Press, 2012, and Gershom Scholem's *Major Trends in Jewish Mysticism*, New York: Schocken Books, 1961.

I spoke with Fred Jennings by phone.

Phil Hine quote from his online article "Evocaton Without Sniffles," available at http://www.philhine.org.uk/writings/sp_evocsniff.html.

Conversation with Rabbi Eyal Riess took place by phone.

Quote from *Forward* article found at https://forward.com/opinion/212064/stephen-hawkings-worst-nightmare-golem-20/.

CHAPTER 2: IN THE (UNCANNY) VALLEY OF THE DOLLS

Interviews with Brittany "Nico" Cox took place in person, with follow-ups by phone and e-mail correspondence.

Alister E. McGrath quote from his book *Science and Religion: A New Introduction*, Hoboken, NJ: John Wiley & Sons, 2011.

Mark Twain quote from his book *Innocents Abroad*, Hartford, CT: American Publishing Company, 1869, available via http://gutenberg.org.

E. T. A. Hoffmann's story "The Sandman" found in *Tales of E. T. A. Hoffmann*, translated by Leonard J. Kent and Elizabeth C. Knight, Chicago: University of Chicago Press, 1974.

The Uncanny by Sigmund Freud is a translation by David McLintock, London: Penguin, 2003.

Frances Yates quote from her essential book *The Rosicrucian Enlightenment*, Abingdon, UK: Routledge, 2000.

Details and quotes about church automata found in Jessica Riskin, "Machines in the Garden," *Republic of Letters* Vol. 2, 1, 2002.

Quote and historical material on automatons from Minsoo Kang, *Sublime Dreams of Living Machines: The Automaton in the European Imagination*, Cambridge, MA: Harvard University Press, 2011.

Harry Houdini's tale of Henri-Louis Jaquet-Droz found in his *The Unmasking of Robert-Houndin*, New York: Publishers Printing Company, 1908.

CHAPTER 3: ROUGH MAGIC

My interview with Nate Dendy was over video chat.

History of theater and the quote by Edith Hall is from her excellent *Greek Tragedy: Suffering Under the Sun*, Oxford, UK: Oxford University Press, 2010.

Interview with Posner found in Zac Thompson's "Stage Magicians: Good for More Than a Few Tricks," *American Theater*, July/August 2016.

Information on the etymology of the word "magic" from https://plato.stanford .edu/entries/episteme-techne/.

Larry Hickman quote found in his chapter "The Phenomenology of the Quotidian Artifact" in *Technology and Contemporary Life*, Dordrecht, Netherlands: D. Reidel Publishing Company, 1988.

Reginald Scot material directly from *The Discoverie of Witchcraft*, New York: Dover Publications, 1989.

Material on Giambattista della Porta and his texts can be found at Scott L. "Omar" Davis's excellent online resource http://www.faculty.umb.edu/gary_zabel/Courses /Phil%20281b/Philosophy%20of%20Magic/Natural_Magic/jportat5.html.

Newspaper quote on Samri Baldwin found in "The Bewildering Mahatmas," *Burlington Evening Gazette*, January 22, 1897: 5.

The history of Spiritualism has been written about extensively. The two sources I found most helpful and from where I quoted are Ann Braude's masterful work *Radical Spirits: Spiritualism and Women's Rights in Nineteenth-Century America*, Boston: Beacon Press, 1989, and Drew Gilpin Faust's *This Republic of Suffering: Death and the American Civil War*, New York: Alfred A. Knopf, 2008.

The story of "Lieut. Grebble" was found in the *Banner of Light*, October 5, 1861.

Quote from the *Defiance Daily Crescent* found in the article "Spiritualism Exposed," November 8, 1888.

Harry Houdini quotes come directly from his marvelous *A Magician Among the Spirits*, New York: Harper & Brothers, 1924.

Historical material on the Davenport brothers and Pepper's Ghost found in Jim Steinmeyer's *Hiding the Elephant: How Magicians Invented the Impossible and Learned to Disappear*, New York: Da Capo Press, 2004.

Davenport quote from *The Saturday Review of Politics, Literature, Science, Art, and Finance*, London: Saturday Review, Ltd., 1917/1918.

Fred Nadis's essential *Wonder Shows: Performing Science, Magic, and Religion in America*, New Brunswick, NJ: Rutgers University Press, 2005, was the source for material on stage magic and Spiritualism.

Much of the Johann Georg Schröpfer story was found in the wonderful book by Nikolaï Mikhaïlovich Karamzin, *Letters of a Russian Traveler, 1789–1790: An Account of a Young Russian Gentleman's Tour Through Germany, Switzerland, France, and England*, New York: Columbia University Press, 1957.

Quote describing Roberts's phantasmagoria found in Albert A. Hopkins's *Magic, Stage Illusions and Scientific Diversions, Including Trick Photography*, London: Samson Low, Marston and Company Limited, 1897, available online at https://www.gutenberg.org/files/45235/45235-h/45235-h.htm.

The Pepper's Ghost patent, "Improvement in apparatus for producing optical illusions," can be viewed in full at https://www.google.com/patents/US221605.

Scottish rite material from Wendy Rae Waszut-Barrett's unpublished doctoral thesis "Scenic Shifts Upon the Scottish Rite Stage: Designing for Masonic Theatre, 1859–1929," May 2009, and C. Lance Brockman's *Theatre of the Fraternity: Staging the Ritual Space of the Scottish Rite of Freemasonry, 1896–1929*, Minneapolis; Jackson, MS: Frederick R. Weisman Art Museum, University of Minnesota, Distributed by University Press of Mississippi, 1996.

Quotes from Ferdinando Buscema are from several interviews over video chat.

Historical information on Giordano Bruno and related quotes from Frances Amelia Yates's *Giordano Bruno and the Hermetic Tradition*, London: Routledge, 2002; Ingrid D. Rowland's *Giordano Bruno: Philosopher/Heretic*, New York: Farrar, Straus and Giroux, 2016; and Liberty Stanavage's "Such a Sinner of His Memory: Prospero, Bruno, and the Failures of Neo-Platonic Memory Magic," *Staging the Superstitions of Early Modern Europe*, eds. Verena Theile and Andrew D. McCarthy, London: Routledge, 2016.

The Kybalion quotes from *The Kybalion*, New York: Jeremy P. Tarcher, 2011.

Peter Carroll's ideas on chaos magic are from his essay "The Magic of Chaos," found at http://www.philhine.org.uk/writings/ess_mach.html.

Other information on Peter Carroll found in Colin Duggan, "Perennialism and Iconoclasm: Chaos Magick and the Legitimacy of Innovation," *Contemporary Esotericism*, New York: Routledge, 2012.

Quote by Allison Kavey on Francis Bacon is found in her *Books of Secrets: Natural Philosophy in England*, 1550–1600, Urbana: University of Illinois Press, 2007.

Rudolf Steiner quote from his essay "The Balance in the World and Man, Lucifer and Ahriman," available through the Rudolf Steiner Archives, http://wn.rsar chive.org/Lectures/GA158/English/RSPC1948/19141120p01.html.

Gareth Branwyn and I corresponded over e-mail.

Story of the Balsamo performance found in J. L. Peabody's "Spirit Pictures and a Speaking Skull," *Popular Mechanics*, June 1963.

CHAPTER 4: THE GHOST AND MS. TAGGART

Interviews with Shannon Taggart took place in person, with follow-ups by phone, video chat, and e-mail correspondence.

A number of wonderful Spiritualist texts are available in the public domain. The ones quoted from include: William Cleveland, *The Religion of Modern Spiritualism Compared with the Christian Religion and its Miracles*, Cincinnati: Light of Truth Publishing Company, 1896; James Coates, *Seeing the Invisible*, London: L.N. Fowler & Co., 1922; Horace Leaf, *What Is This Spiritualism?* New York: George H. Doran Company, 1919; E. Wilmot Sprague, *Spirit Mediumship*, Detroit: Rev. E. W. Sprague, 1912; J. Coates, *Photographing the Invisible*, London: L.N. Fowler & Co., 1911.

Arthur Conan Doyle quotes are from his *The Coming of the Fairies*, New York: The George H. Doran Company, 1922, available online at https://archive.org /details/comingoffairies00doylrich.

Max Weber on Protestantism found in his *The Protestant Ethic and the Spirit of Capitalism*, Kettering, OH: Angelico Press, 2014.

Ann Braude quote from *Radical Spirits*.

Spiritualist newspapers quoted from include the July 1897 issue of the Spiritualist journal *Borderland*, and the November 1, 1862, issue of the *Banner of Light*.

Material on Mumler and Hudson is from two excellent sources: Louis Kaplan, *The Strange Case of William Mumler, Spirit Photographer*, Minneapolis: University of Minnesota Press, 2008, and Clement Cheroux and Metropolitan Museum of Art, *The Perfect Medium: Photography and the Occult*, New Haven, CT: Yale University Press, 2005.

Material on Alfred Russel Wallace and Eleanor Mildred Sidgwick found in *Proceedings of the Society of Psychical Research* VII, 1891–1892.

Material on the aura goggles from Francis J. Rebman, *The Human Aura*, Storm Lake, IA, 1912.

Material on Schrenck-Notzing is from his book *Phenomena of Materialisation*, London: E. P. Dutton & Company, 1920. Other sources include J. D. Beresford, "More New Facts in Psychical Research," *Harper's Magazine*, March 1922, and John Harvey, *Photography and Spirit*, London: Reaktion Books, 2007.

CHAPTER 5: GUIDED BY VOICES

Interviews with Donna Hogan were over video chat and e-mail correspondence.

Historical material on the "spiritual telegraph" and quote from Bret E. Carroll, *Spiritualism in Antebellum America*, Bloomington: Indiana University Press, 1997.

Details on the magazine *The Unexplained* are from an e-mail correspondence with Peter Brookesmith.

Konstanin Raudive is quoted directly from his book *Breakthrough: An Amazing Experiment in Electronic Communication with the Dead*, New York: Taplinger, 1971, and his recordings were graciously made available to me by Buried Treasure Records, who provided me with a digital copy of *Breakthrough*, Vista Production Recording, 1971.

Friedrich Jürgenson material is from Joe Banks, *Rorschach Audio: Art and Illusion for Sound*, London: Strange Attractor Press, 2012 (which is quoted throughout), and the compact disc release *Friedrich Jürgenson From the Studio for Audioscopic Research*, Ash International, 2000.

Vladimir Bogoraz quotes and material are from his journals published in *Memoirs of the American Natural History Museum, Volume IX*, Leiden, Netherlands: E.J. Brill Ltd., 1904.

Article on George Meek is from Henry David Rosso, "'Dial-the-Dead' TV Coming Soon, Researchers Insist," *Harrisburg Daily Register*, April 7, 1982.

Anthony Sanchez, the developer of Ethereal, answered some questions over e-mail.

Historical material on the Ouija board is from the essential Mitch Horowitz, *Occult America*, reprint edition, New York: Bantam, 2010.

Dee quotes are from *A True and Faithful Relation of What Passed for Many Years Between Dr. John Dee and Some Spirits*, a facsimile of which can be found at https://quod.lib.umich.edu/e/eebo/A37412.0001.001/1:15?rgn=div1;view

=fulltext. Dee's quote describing his stone is found in Benjamin Woolley's *The Queen's Conjurer: The Science and Magic of Dr. John Dee, Advisor to Queen Elizabeth I*, New York: Henry Holt and Company, 2001. Details on Joseph Smith's use of seeing stones is from the momentous work of D. Michael Quinn, *Early Mormonism and the Magic World View*, Salt Lake City, UT: Signature Books, 1998. Also quoted in this section is Ogden Kraut's "Seers and Seer Stones," accessed at http://ogdenkraut.com/?page_id=191.

CHAPTER 6: "IN A LIGHT FANTASTIC ROUND"

Title for this chapter is from John Milton's 1634 masque *Comus* and is believed to be the origin of the term "tripping the light fantastic."

Interview with Ronni Thomas was in person, with some clarifications over e-mail.

David Lynch profile by Claire Hoffman is found in "David Lynch Is Back . . . as a Guru of Transcendental Meditation," *The New York Times Magazine*, February 22, 2013.

Robert Monroe's patents can be seen in full at https://www.google.com/patents/US5356368 and https://www.google.com/patents/US3884218. Hemi-Sync trademark quote can be found at http://tmsearch.uspto.gov/bin/showfield?f=doc& state=4806:joe7r8.2.9.

Robert Monroe's books from which I quoted and used for background material include: *Journeys Out of the Body*, Garden City, New York: Doubleday & Company, 1971; *Far Journeys*, New York: Main Street Books, 1985; *Ultimate Journey*, New York: Broadway Books, 2000.

Rosalind A. McKnight quotes are from her book *Cosmic Journeys: My Out-of-Body Explorations with Robert A. Monroe*, Charlottesville, VA: Hampton Roads Publishing Company, 1999.

Historical material and quotes related to the Dreamachine from several sources: Laura Hoptman and John Geiger, *Brion Gysin: Dream Machine*, London/New York: Merrell Publishers/New Museum, 2010; John Geiger, *Chapel of Extreme Experience*, Toronto: Gutter Press, 2002; Klarion the Witch Boy, "Dream On: Looking Again at the Dreamachine," *Headpress* 25, 2003.

Quote from Andrew McKenzie is from the booklet included in the CD set *The Hafler Trio & Thee Temple Ov Psychick Youth – Present Brion Gysin's Dreamachine*, KK Records, 1989.

W. Grey Walter quote from his book *The Living Brain*, Harmondsworth, UK: Penguin Books, 1968.

Material on theta states and hypnagogia is from Michelle Carr, "How to Dream Like Salvador Dalí," *Psychology Today* 20, February 2015, https://www.psychology today.com/blog/dream-factory/201502/how-dream-salvador-dali, and Thomas Budzynski, "The Clinical Guide to Sound and Light," http://www.amadeux .net/sublimen/documenti/REF_clinicalguide.pdf.

Interview with Mitch Altman took place over video chat.

Material on Aldous Huxley from my own book *Too Much to Dream: A Psychedelic American Boyhood*, New York: Soft Skull Press, 2011, and my article "Getting There Too Quickly: Aldous Huxley and Mescaline," *The Revealer*, January 2, 2012, and directly from his *Doors of Perception, and Heaven and Hell*, New York: Harper & Row, 1963.

Some information on transhumanism and quotes are from: Meghan O'Gieblyn, "God in the Machine: My Strange Journey into Transhumanism," TheGuardian .com, April 18, 2017; Kevin O'Neill, *Internet Afterlife: Virtual Salvation in the 21st Century*, Santa Barbara, CA: Praeger, 2016; Edward Regis, *Great Mambo Chicken and the Transhuman Condition: Science Slightly over the Edge*, Reading, MA: Addison-Wesley Publishing Company, 1993; and Mark Gubrud, "Why Transhumanism Won't Work," *The New Atlantis*, June 2010, http://fu turisms.thenewatlantis.com/2010/06/why-transhumanism-wont-work.html.

Samuel Watson quote from *The Religion of Spiritualism: Its Phenomena and Philosophy*, Boston: Colby & Rich, 1889.

CHAPTER 7: FEAR AND SOLDERING

The "Spooky Tesla Spirit Radio" project can be found at https://www.instructa bles.com/id/Spooky-Tesla-Spirit-Radio/.

Material on Tesla from a number of excellent sources: Margaret Cheney, *Tesla: Man Out of Time*, New York: Simon & Schuster, 2001; W. Bernard Carlson, *Tesla: Inventor of the Electrical Age*, Princeton, NJ: Princeton University Press, 2015; and John J. O'Neill, *Prodigal Genius: The Life of Nikola Tesla*, Kempton, IL: Adventures Unlimited Press, 2008.

Unarius material on Tesla found at their website http://www.teslaenergy.org /intro1.html.

The wonderful *Popular Electronics* article and related letters are found in Konstantinos, "Ghost Voices," *Popular Electronics*, October 1995, and "Letters," *Popular Electronics*, February 1996, both of which are available as PDFs online at http://www.americanradiohistory.com/Popular-Electronics-Guide.htm.

History and quotes related to Frank Sumption are from a number of online sources including: Tim Woolworth, "Frank Sumption: Frank's Box Creator and the Father of the Ghost Box," *ITC Voices* 6, February 2011, http://itcvoices .org/frank-sumption-franks-box-creator-and-the-father-of-the-ghost-box/.

Karen Stollznow, "Frank's Box: The Broken Radio," *Committee for Skeptical Inquiry* 28, January 2010, http://www.csicop.org/specialarticles/show/franks _box_the_broken_radio.

Karen Stollznow, "Let's Be Frank (Sumption)," *Skepchick* 5, January 2010, http:// skepchick.org/2010/01/lets-be-frank-sumption/.

Quote from Jenny Hazelgrove found in *Spiritualism and British Society between the Wars*, Manchester, UK: Manchester University Press, 2000.

Quotes from Jacques Vallée are from his delightful book *Dimensions: A Casebook of Alien Contact*, San Antonio, TX: Anomalist Books, 2008.

Quotes from Kim Cascone are from his article "Errormancy: Glitch as Divination," *The End of Being*, April 19, 2012, http://theendofbeing.com/2012/04/19 /errormancy-glitch-as-divination-a-new-essay-by-kim-cascone/, and over e-mail.

Two highly recommended sources on supernatural and related phenomena I found useful are George P. Hansen, *The Trickster and the Paranormal*, Philadelphia: Xlibris Corporation, 2001; and Whitley Strieber and Jeffrey Kripal, *The Super Natural: A New Vision of the Unexplained*, New York: TarcherPerigee, 2017.

Michael Winkelman and John R. Baker, *Supernatural as Natural: A Biocultural Approach to Religion*, London: Routledge, 2010.

Acknowledgments

Inexpressible thanks to Mitch Horowitz, who seems to think in my weird ideas are the seeds of books. Your support and continued faith mean the world to me. Thanks to my agent, Matthew Elblonk, who often plays therapist. Your counsel is always spot-on, and I am so grateful to have you in my corner. I'm also extremely grateful to Nina Shield who came to the project late but has wisely steered the ship the rest of the way.

There were many folks who helped make this possible, but the biggest thanks go out to those people who allowed me to profile them for this work through numerous interviews in person, phone calls, video chats, and follow-up e-mails. All my gratitude to Donna Hogan, Nico Cox, Ferdinando Buscema, Joshua Madara, Ronni Thomas, Mitch Altman, Nate Dendy, Rabbi Eyal Riess, and most especially Shannon Taggart, whose insights, friendship, and creative genius have fueled this book from start to finish. Other folks who offered their time and ideas include Kim Cascone, Steve Hultay, Ron Nagy, Kevin LaGrandeur,

ACKNOWLEDGMENTS

Anthony Sanchez, Fred Jennings, Gal Sofer, and my dear friend Stephen Hazan Arnoff. Special thanks to Mark Podwal and CM von Hausswolff.

My work in general is supported by an incredible network of people, and this book in particular had several spiritual advisors, people who over the years have become some of my dearest friends: the fabulous Pam Grossman, a kindred soul of infinite worlds; Gareth Branwyn, my brother from another mother and twentieth-level magic-user; and Mark Pilkington, one of the most extraordinary fellows I have had the pleasure of knowing. My great pal Joe Gallo as always was a stalwart supporter.

To the whole host of my dear family friends, but a special shout-out to Ezra Glenn, Seth Riskin, Jason Patch and family, Ethan Gilsdorf, Janaka Stucky, JP Gluting, and Scott Korb for continued writerly companionship. Also thanks to Jamie Sutcliffe (the man I most want to play RPGs with), Robert Ansell, and William Kiesel. To the Neill/Armsby clan, my sisters Karen and Lisa. Forever missing my mother, Ruth; my father, Byron; and my brother, Eric.

Index

INDEX

About the Author

Peter Bebergal is the author of *Season of the Witch, The Faith Between Us* (with Scott Korb), and *Too Much to Dream: A Psychedelic American Boyhood*. He writes widely on the speculative and slightly fringe, and essays and reviews have appeared in *The Times Literary Supplement, Boing Boing, The Believer*, and *The Quietus*. He studied religion and culture at Harvard Divinity School. He lives in Cambridge, Massachusetts, with his wife and son.